Couples Therapy:
Feminist Perspectives

Couples Therapy: Feminist Perspectives

Marcia Hill, EdD
Esther D. Rothblum, PhD
Editors

Couples Therapy: Feminist Perspectives, edited by Marcia Hill and Esther D. Rothblum, was simultaneously issued by The Haworth Press, Inc., under the same title, as a special issue of the journal *Women & Therapy,* Volume 19, Number 3 1996, Marcia Hill and Esther D. Rothblum, Editors.

Harrington Park Press
An Imprint of
The Haworth Press, Inc.
New York • London

ISBN 1-56023-094-0

Published by

Harrington Park Press, 10 Alice Street, Binghamton, NY 13904-1580 USA

Harrington Park Press is an imprint of The Haworth Press, Inc., 10 Alice Street, Binghamton, NY 13904-1580 USA

Couples Therapy: Feminist Perspectives has also been published as *Women & Therapy*, Volume 19, Number 3 1996.

The development, preparation, and publication of this work has been undertaken with great care. However, the publisher, employees, editors, and agents of The Haworth Press and all imprints of The Haworth Press, Inc., including The Haworth Medical Press and Pharmaceutical Products Press, are not responsible for any errors contained herein or for consequences that may ensue from use of materials or information contained in this work. Opinions expressed by the author(s) are not necessarily those of The Haworth Press, Inc.

Library of Congress Cataloging-in-Publication Data

Couples therapy : feminist perspectives / Marcia Hill, Esther D. Rothblum, editors.
    p. cm.
  Includes bibliographical references.
    ISBN 0-7890-0017-2 (alk. paper). –ISBN 1-56023-094-0 (alk. paper)
    1. Marital psychotherapy. 2. Feminist therapy. 3. Cultural psychiatry. 4. Lesbians–Mental health services. I. Hill, Marcia. II. Rothblum, Esther D.
RC488.5.C6438 1996
616.89'156–dc21
          96-39368
          CIP

INDEXING & ABSTRACTING

Contributions to this publication are selectively indexed or abstracted in print, electronic, online, or CD-ROM version(s) of the reference tools and information services listed below. This list is current as of the copyright date of this publication. See the end of this section for additional notes.

- *Abstracts of Research in Pastoral Care & Counseling*, Loyola College, 7135 Minstrel Way, Suite 101, Columbia, MD 21045

- *Academic Abstracts/CD-ROM,* EBSCO Publishing Editorial Department, P.O. Box 590, Ipswich, MA 01938-0590

- *Academic Index (on-line),* Information Access Company, 362 Lakeside Drive, Foster City, CA 94404

- *Alternative Press Index*, Alternative Press Center, Inc., P.O. Box 33109, Baltimore, MD 21218-0401

- *Behavioral Medicine Abstracts*, University of Washington, School of Social Work, Seattle, WA 98195

- *CNPIEC Reference Guide: Chinese National Directory of Foreign Periodicals*, P.O. Box 88, Beijing, People's Republic of China

- *Current Contents: Clinical Medicine/Life Sciences (CC: CM/LS) (weekly Table of Contents Service), and Social Science Citation Index. Articles also searchable through Social SciSearch, ISI's online database and in ISI's Research Alert current awareness service*, Institute for Scientific Information, 3501 Market Street, Philadelphia, PA 19104-3302 (USA)

- *Digest of Neurology and Psychiatry*, The Institute of Living, 400 Washington Street, Hartford, CT 06106

- *Expanded Academic Index,* Information Access Company, 362 Lakeside Drive, Forest City, CA 94404

- *Family Studies Database (online and CD/ROM),* National Information Services Corporation, 306 East Baltimore Pike, 2nd Floor, Media, PA 19063

- *Family Violence & Sexual Assault Bulletin*, Family Violence & Sexual Assault Institute, 1310 Clinic Drive, Tyler, TX 75701

- *Feminist Periodicals: A Current Listing of Contents*, Women's Studies Librarian-at-Large, 728 State Street, 430 Memorial Library, Madison, WI 53706

- *Health Source: Indexing & Abstracting of 160 selected health related journals, updated monthly:* EBSCO Publishing, 83 Pine Street, Peabody, MA 01960

- *Health Source Plus: expanded version of "Health Source" to be released shortly:* EBSCO Publishing, 83 Pine Street, Peabody, MA 01960

- *Higher Education Abstracts*, Claremont Graduate School, 231 East Tenth Street, Claremont, CA 91711

(continued)

- *IBZ International Bibliography of Periodical Literature*, Zeller Verlag GmbH & Co, P.O.B. 1949, d-49009 Osnabruck, Germany

- *Index to Periodical Articles Related to Law*, University of Texas, 727 East 26th Street, Austin, TX 78705

- *INTERNET ACCESS (& additional networks) Bulletin Board for Libraries ("BUBL"), coverage of information resources on INTERNET, JANET, and other networks.*
  - JANET X.29: UK.AC.BATH.BUBL or 00006012101300
  - TELNET: BUBL.BATH.AC.UK or 138.38.32.45 login 'bubl'
  - Gopher: BUBL.BATH.AC.UK (138.32.32.45). Port 7070
  - World Wide Web: http: / / www.bubl.bath.ac.uk./BUBL/ home.html
  - NISSWAIS: telnetniss.ac.uk (for the NISS gateway)
  The Andersonian Library, Curran Building, 101 St. James Road, Glasgow G4 ONS, Scotland

- *Mental Health Abstracts (online through DIALOG)*, IFI/Plenum Data Company, 3202 Kirkwood Highway, Wilmington, DE 19808

- *ONS Nursing Scan in Oncology–NAACOG's Women's Health Nursing Scan*, NURSECOM, Inc., 1211 Locust Street, Philadelphia, PA 19107

- *PASCAL International Bibliography T205: Sciences de l'information Documentation*, INIST/CNRS-Service Gestion des Documents Primaires, 2, allee du Parc de Brabois, F-54514 Vandoeuvre-les-Nancy, Cedex, France

- *Periodical Abstracts, Research I* (general & basic reference indexing & abstracting data-base from University Microfilms International (UMI), 300 North Zeeb Road, P.O. Box 1346, Ann Arbor, MI 48106-1346), UMI Data Courier, P.O. Box 32770, Louisville, KY 40232-2770

- *Periodical Abstracts, Research II* (broad coverage indexing & abstracting data-base from University Microfilms International (UMI), 300 North Zeeb Road, P.O. Box 1346, Ann Arbor, MI 48106-1346), UMI Data Courier, P.O. Box 32770, Louisville, KY 40232-2770

- *Psychological Abstracts (PsycINFO)*, American Psychological Association, P.O. Box 91600, Washington, DC 20090-1600

- *Published International Literature on Traumatic Stress (The PILOTS Database)*, National Center for Post-Traumatic Stress Disorder (116 D), VA Medical Center, White River Junction, VT 05009

- *Sage Family Studies Abstracts (SFSA)*, Sage Publications, Inc., 2455 Teller Road, Newbury Park, CA 91320

- *Social Work Abstracts*, National Association of Social Workers, 750 First Street NW, 8th Floor, Washington, DC 20002

- *Studies on Women Abstracts*, Carfax Publishing Company, P.O. Box 25, Abingdon, Oxfordshire OX14 3UE, United Kingdom

(continued)

- *Violence and Abuse Abstracts: A Review of Current Literature on Interpersonal Violence (VAA)*, Sage Publications, Inc., 2455 Teller Road, Newbury Park, CA 91320

- *Women Studies Abstracts*, Rush Publishing Company, P.O. Box 1, Rush, NY 14543

- *Women's Studies Index (indexed comprehensively)*, G. K. Hall & Co., 1633 Broadway, 5th Floor, New York, NY 10019

SPECIAL BIBLIOGRAPHIC NOTES

related to special journal issues (separates) and indexing/abstracting

☐ indexing/abstracting services in this list will also cover material in any "separate" that is co-published simultaneously with Haworth's special thematic journal issue or DocuSerial. Indexing/abstracting usually covers material at the article/chapter level.

☐ monographic co-editions are intended for either non-subscribers or libraries which intend to purchase a second copy for their circulating collections.

☐ monographic co-editions are reported to all jobbers/wholesalers/approval plans. The source journal is listed as the "series" to assist the prevention of duplicate purchasing in the same manner utilized for books-in-series.

☐ to facilitate user/access services all indexing/abstracting services are encouraged to utilize the co-indexing entry note indicated at the bottom of the first page of each article/chapter/contribution.

☐ this is intended to assist a library user of any reference tool (whether print, electronic, online, or CD-ROM) to locate the monographic version if the library has purchased this version but not a subscription to the source journal.

☐ individual articles/chapters in any Haworth publication are also available through the Haworth Document Delivery Services (HDDS).

CONTENTS

Foreword   xi
    Marcia Hill

Unsexing the Couple   1
    Marny Hall

Cultural Considerations in Couples Therapy   13
    Pamela A. Hays

Loving Across Race and Class Divides: Relational
    Challenges and the Interracial Lesbian Couple   25
    Sarah F. Pearlman

The Narrative/Collaborative Process in Couples Therapy:
    A Postmodern Perspective   37
    Diane T. Gottlieb
    Charles D. Gottlieb

African American Lesbian Couples: Ethnocultural
    Considerations in Psychotherapy   49
    Beverly Greene
    Nancy Boyd-Franklin

The Use of *Voice* for Assessment and Intervention
    in Couples Therapy   61
    Janet M. Sims

Intimate Partners: A Context for the Intensification
    and Healing of Emotional Pain   79
    Maryhelen Snyder

From Isolation to Mutuality: A Feminist Collaborative
    Model of Couples Therapy   93
    Karen Skerrett

ABOUT THE EDITORS

Marcia Hill, EdD, is a feminist therapist in private practice in Montpelier, Vermont. She also does consulting, writing, and teaching in the areas of feminist therapy theory and practice. She is a member and past Chair of the Feminist Therapy Institute. Marcia has been involved in grassroots political work for almost 20 years, including helping to start a shelter for battered women. Her free time is spent gardening, backpacking, and maintaining a home in a rural area.

Esther D. Rothblum, PhD, is Professor in the Department of Psychology at the University of Vermont. She was the recipient of a Kellogg Fellowship that involved travel to Africa to study women's mental health. Her research and writing have focused on mental health disorders in which women predominate, including depression, the social stigma of women's weight, procrastination and fear of failure, and women in the Antarctic. She has co-edited 21 books, including *Another Silenced Trauma: Twelve Feminist Therapists and Activists Respond to One Woman's Recovery From War*, which won a Distinguished Publication Award from the Association for Women in Psychology.

Foreword

Working with couples has long been a challenge to therapists. The art of psychotherapy was, after all, founded both theoretically and practically in the domain of the individual. Making the leap from individual to couples therapy involves more than simply including a third person in the session.

When I was a green therapist, I did just that: tried to do couples therapy by doing individual therapy with two people at once. It seemed to me that if both individuals were "healthy," whatever that meant, then their relationship would be healthy as well. Before long, it was distressingly obvious that while this process may have helped in a minor way, it truly was the wrong tool for the job. I still think that there is a modicum of truth to the "healthy people make healthy relationships" theory, but I no longer assume that individual well-being is the primary goal of couples therapy. It may be a welcomed–and perhaps even predictable–side effect, perhaps, but not necessarily more than that.

The interplay between the state of the individual and that of the couple is complex. On the one hand, much of what brings couples to a therapist's office is some form of projection, assumptions learned early in life about what is possible or dangerous in the give-and-take of relationships. Yet, as I often tell my clients, none of us make it to adulthood without scars and neurotic quirks. Even the most intact and insightful of us retain some old pain, some tender spots that occasionally intrude into our lives. And most of us, nonetheless, manage to form a range of connections with coworkers, friends, neighbors and family.

[Haworth co-indexing entry note]: "Foreword." Hill, Marcia. Co-published simultaneously in *Women & Therapy* (The Haworth Press, Inc.) Vol. 19, No. 3, 1996, pp. xiii-xv; and: *Couples Therapy: Feminist Perspectives* (ed: Marcia Hill and Esther D. Rothblum) The Haworth Press, Inc., 1996, pp. xiii-xv; and: *Couples Therapy: Feminist Perspectives* (ed: Marcia Hill and Esther D. Rothblum) Harrington Park Press, an imprint of The Haworth Press, Inc., 1996, pp. xi-xiii. Single or multiple copies of this article are available for a fee from The Haworth Document Delivery Service [1-800-342-9678, 9:00 a.m. - 5:00 p.m. (EST). E-mail address: getinfo@haworth.com].

The goal of couples therapy, then, is not somehow to help both individuals become so enlightened that their distress no longer interferes with the couple relationship, although sometimes one or the other in the pair may need to attend to some particularly intrusive aspect of their hurt. The goal, rather, is to help the couple find a way to accommodate and appreciate one another's uniqueness in the entire range from what is difficult and painful to what feels easy and pleasurable. In fact, ideally one hopes that the couple will eventually blur the line between those two poles, so that each comes to feel tenderly toward or charmed by or even a relaxed detachment in response to the aspects of the other that used to seem so problematic. When couples move back into alliance, those kinds of responses, which would have seemed wildly impossible when they started couples therapy, often can come naturally. After all, most couples did feel that way about one another's foibles early in their relationship.

For the feminist therapist, the literature about working with couples has often been disappointing. Much of what is available assumes that all couples are heterosexual and white, often assuming as well that such couples have or should have children, are able-bodied, and in general fit therapists' notions of mainstream America. It is not surprising that couples who do not fit this profile have historically been reluctant to seek out therapy for relationship difficulties. And perhaps that reluctance has been just as well, given that therapists often have been ill-prepared to respond effectively to a more diverse clientele.

Most of what is written about couples therapy has also failed to take cultural context and matters of power into account. For heterosexual couples in particular, this has been a glaring and sometimes dangerous omission. Therapists used to respond to battering in a relationship by attempting to attribute equal responsibility to both partners, ignoring the realities for the woman of her (generally speaking) smaller physical size, economic dependence, and social constraints; ignoring as well the man's assumed prerogative to get his way, by bullying if necessary. Thankfully, this kind of blatant disregard for power inequities is increasingly rare. Inattention to the more subtle aspects of power and privilege as they are played out in couple relationships is, however, still almost universal.

In this collection, some of these omissions and inadequacies have been addressed. Race and ethnicity as well as sexual orientation, especially, are spoken to by several authors. And all authors offer a perspective that is grounded in an appreciation of cultural context, the effects of privilege, and the centrality of a respectful stance on the part of the therapist. It is a valuable compilation which we hope will prove useful to any therapist seeking to do informed and re-sponsive work with couples in distress.

Marcia Hill

Unsexing the Couple

Marny Hall

SUMMARY. Frequently, long-term lesbian couples who have little or no sex seek therapeutic help for their "problem." Rather than treating "lesbian bed death," those of us who work with such lesbian couples need to examine our own pro-sex biases and to start educating ourselves and our clients about the normalcy of nongenital intimacy between long-term lesbian partners. This article offers specific suggestions for combating culturally-conditioned celibaphobia in ourselves and our clients. *[Article copies available for a fee from The Haworth Document Delivery Service: 1-800-342-9678. E-mail address: getinfo@haworth.com]*

"But does it count?" My lesbian client perches anxiously on the edge of her chair, waiting for reassurance. If she can be certain that the vibrator-induced orgasms she has with her lover constitute "real" sex, she can relax. At least for the moment, she has kept the dreaded epidemic at bay.

Lesbian bed death, the infamous condition that my client is so apprehensive about, was officially documented in 1983. After sur-

---

Marny Hall, LCSW, PhD, a Bay Area lesbian psychotherapist for the last twenty years, has encouraged lesbians to enjoy everything from insane passion to serene celibacy. She is the author of *The Lavender Couch: A Consumer's Guide to Psychotherapy for Lesbians and Gay Men*.

Address correspondence to: Marny Hall, LCSW, PhD, 4112 24th Street, San Francisco, CA 94114.

[Haworth co-indexing entry note]: "Unsexing the Couple." Hall, Marny. Co-published simultaneously in *Women & Therapy* (The Haworth Press, Inc.) Vol. 19, No. 3, 1996, pp. 1-11; and: *Couples Therapy: Feminist Perspectives* (ed: Marcia Hill and Esther D. Rothblum) The Haworth Press, Inc., 1996, pp. 1-11; and: *Couples Therapy: Feminist Perspectives* (ed: Marcia Hill and Esther D. Rothblum) Harrington Park Press, an imprint of The Haworth Press, Inc., 1996, pp. 1-11. Single or multiple copies of this article are available for a fee from The Haworth Document Delivery Service [1-800-342-9678, 9:00 a.m. - 5:00 p.m. (EST). E-mail address: getinfo@haworth.com].

veying thousands of couples with varying sexual preferences, researchers Richard Blumstein and Pepper Schwartz concluded that long-term lesbian couples have substantially less sex than either their heterosexual or male homosexual counterparts.

In the decade after *American Couples* (Blumstein & Schwartz, 1983) was published, lesbian sexual mores underwent many radical changes. But despite butch/femme liberation, soaring dildo sales, and the proliferation of lesbian sex clubs and parties in the nineties, lesbians appear to retain the dubious distinction of being sexual underachievers. A comparison between a major national study of non-homosexuals and a survey of two thousand lesbians suggests that after only two years together, lesbians have sex less frequently than married heterosexual couples do after ten years. And more than two thirds of all the lesbians surveyed in the study said they want more frequent sexual contact (Lever, 1995).

Perhaps so much outspokenness about lesbian sex–even its disappointing aspects–is a positive sign. After all, grousing about girlfriends in a public forum would have been unthinkable for women who, just a few decades ago, dared not even whisper the l-word. But, despite the increased tolerance of homosexuality, and the new sense of entitlement that has accompanied it, many of the early goals of Gay Liberation remain unrealized. Gay partnerships, for example, have yet to gain formal, and in many instances, informal recognition.

As long as the outside world wavers about the legitimacy of same-sex marriages, women partners will have to rely on their own self-generated measures of validity. In this context of invisibility, my client's question about vibrator orgasms makes sense. With societal affirmations of gay relationships in short supply, an active sex life may seem to be all that separates a real lesbian from–according to a joke currently making the rounds–a hasbian.

SOCIAL PROBLEMS IN CLINICAL SETTINGS

It is easy to see how the perception of inadequate sexuality is formed among lesbians. When it comes to same-sex unions, many families are mute or disapproving; and, given the current political climate, hopes of shoring up gay civil rights seem more and more remote. There is, however, one glimmer of recognition emanating from the mainstream.

For the last century, sociologists, sexologists and psychologists have named and analyzed homosexuality, theorized about same-sex coupling and, in some cases, even pleaded the cause of gay rights. Thankful for any mention of their lives, lesbians have frequently overlooked the phallocentric biases that underpin such research and theory.

The renegade psychologist, R. D. Laing, summed up the lure of social science nicely. It is lonely and painful to be misunderstood, he wrote. But to be understood "is also to be in danger of being engulfed, when the 'understanding' occurs within a framework that one had hoped to break out of" (1970, p. 76).

Sex surveys like those of Blumstein and Schwartz, while acknowledging the importance of sex between women, fail to measure the ongoing, affectionate, physical, but nongenital exchanges—the spooning and cuddling, the playful hugs and intimate conversations—that first-person accounts of lesbian couples so often reveal. The relentless quantification of what "counts" in sex surveys and other research, no matter how well-intentioned, does not begin to illuminate the nature of many lesbian relationships. However, such tallies, which add another strand to the preexisting layers of self-doubt, are gratefully and often uncritically consumed by lesbians hungry for any reflection of their lives.

It is the ultimate irony: lesbians, diagnosed as mentally ill twenty years ago because they had sex with other women, are now deemed unhealthy because they don't. And the psychologists who have contributed to the problem are there with the remedy—this time, in the form of sex therapy.

SEXUAL PRESENTING PROBLEMS: CHALLENGING THE FRAME

It is a common scenario: worried about diminishing desire, a lesbian couple seeks therapy. Rather than challenging the couple's assertion that something is "wrong" with their sex life, therapists have been trained to probe for the underlying "problem." And sure enough, they are likely to find that a discrepancy in desire between the partners correlates with a power imbalance: perhaps the "no" partner feels at a disadvantage socially because her lover has more friends or money. Or, just as commonly, the "yes" partner feels unloved or somehow inadequate. If therapists help clients sound off about such imbalances, family-systems experts theorize that sex will return to healthy *status quo ante* levels (Weeks & Hof, 1987). But the articulation of such inequities, much as it may help partners mention the unmentionable, does not correct them. Neither the fortunes or charisma of the more endowed partner, nor the insecurity of her mate, is likely to change in the near future. Nor is their discrepant desire. Frequently, such couples terminate therapy feeling "uncured" and doubly-derelict—failures at both sex *and* sex therapy.

Diminished or discrepant sexual desire may or may not be related to other inequities in the partnership. But, to give the systems theorists the benefit of the doubt for just a moment, let's say it is. Why should couples' therapists automatically assume that redressing these imbalances in the bedroom is necessarily undesirable? Perhaps discrepant sexual desire is itself desirable—the most sensible way of settling other scores, and thereby achieving the overall relationship parity that is so highly prized by lesbian couples (Huston & Schwartz, 1995).

Of course, inequality, in or out of the bedroom, is not the issue for many couples. Perhaps the therapist uncovers some evidence that the client experienced early sexual trauma. Again, theory has it that if clients "work through" such residual pain, sex will flourish again (Weeks & Hof, 1987). But rather than early memories inhibiting present-day sex, could the internalized lesbian imperative to "do it" be evoking early memories of "forced" sex? And rather than present-day "no's" being a *symptom* of early trauma, might the refusals actually constitute a healthy reaction to earlier tyrannies?

Such analyses of sexual presenting problems may seem farfetched to us, and even more unpalatable to our clients. But our unwillingness to entertain such alternatives speaks volumes about the power of cultural attitudes and the reverence with which we all, therapists and clients alike, hold sexual activity in couples' relationships. This reverence blinds us to the conclusion that, by now, should be obvious: it is perfectly normal for seasoned lesbian couples to have little or no sex. And what needs to be "fixed" is not long-term partners, but rather the pro-sex zeal of their therapists.

PHYSICIAN, HEAL THYSELF

Like many of my colleagues, I have been trained in the More-Is-Better school of sex therapy. Much as I might want to embrace the notion that sexual tumescence in one's genitals is as incidental as the amount of melanin in one's skin, my reactions give me away. I notice, for instance, that I perk up if partnered clients come in reporting signs of rekindled eroticism. Just as I am disappointed when they report their "failures." Naturally, I try, probably without much success, to appear neutral.

How can I be less invested in my clients' sex lives when I'm anything but casual about my own? Like the couples I work with, I, too, have an internal sex calendar that automatically keeps track of the days since the last time. I am full of sympathetic clucks and suggestions when friends bring up their own cases of lesbian bed death. And the "just" that I almost always append before I utter the word "friend" gives away the fact that I believe nonsexual intimacies are somehow substandard.

Through trial and error, I have devised a regimen that does not eliminate my pro-sex bias, but does continually remind me of alternative perspectives on meaningful intimacy. There are, for example, several books I refer to so religiously that I can justifiably call them my bibles.

In *Friends and Lovers* (1976), anthropologist-author Robert Brain conducts a tour of affectionate bonds through history and across cultures. In *A Passion for Friends* (1986), Brain's lesbian/feminist counterpart, Janice Raymond, examines the nonsexual bonds between women. And finally, Sally Cline, British feminist and academic, explores the same territory from a slightly different angle in *Women, Celibacy and Passion* (1993).

Besides keeping a lookout for other books and articles that elucidate and celebrate the pleasures of celibacy and platonic friendship, I have dinner every Saturday night with a very content, single-by-choice friend who keeps me abreast of the latest research on celibacy and has no qualms about pointing out my bias. ("Why do you refer to me as single?" she asks. "I have a great many important emotional and professional attachments. I'm simply not part of a couple.") I find these corrections to be well-deserved and much-needed consciousness refreshers.

Another part of my regimen is my ongoing search for women whose intimacies are based on nongenital sources of stimulation, pleasure, and well-being. At first, I thought I should focus on bonds between good friends or between ex-lovers. But, upon reflection, I realized that platonic intimacies, by their very definition, only reinforce the power of sex (or its absence) to typecast and rank relationships. Consequently, I decided to look for examples of intimacy that avoid the dichotomous classification of sex or no sex.

Relationships in which sex is neither central nor absent fall into a borderland that could be designated "genital incidentalism" (Hall, 1993). Through various lesbian networks, I have located several genital incidentalists.

Martha and Marcia had, the item in the local gay newspaper read, just celebrated "21 years of open love, uncommitted sex, firm friendship and wild adventures." When I tracked them down, they told me they had met when they were both rookie lesbians. For the next two decades they lived hundreds of miles apart, but periodically they would rendezvous to backpack, gossip, commiserate about breakups, and, when they were in the mood, have sex. Their public celebration was intended as a wake-up call to friends who seemed to overlook their multifaceted relationship.

Leah, another genital incidentalist, also cherished friendly sex. Falling in love, Leah recounted, had landed her in a destructive, long-term relationship. After it was over, she avoided similar entanglements. In contrast, sex with friends with whom she might just as well go to a movie or play bridge, turned out to be unproblematic and sustaining.

Hettie also eschewed conventional relationships. Occasionally she slept with ex-lovers. But she was just as likely to share a meal with them. Their erotic encounters, like their lively dinner conversation, were simply a way to certify continuing rapport.

All these women are unpartnered, yet connected. Since their bonds do not depend on sex, these genital incidentalists are never estranged or anxious about their relationship with each other during nonsexual periods. Putting the genital sex on hold, they can still be social companions or backpacking buddies (Hall, 1995).

Interestingly enough, I stumbled upon a configuration I never expected to find in the genitally incidental category: Corrie, Angela, and Skeeter call themselves "a committed threesome." When they first moved in together five years ago, they decided to have sex only when all three were available and receptive. Since neither their schedules nor their desires are well-synchronized, such a convergence is rare. Nevertheless, they aren't worried about lesbian bed death. "Sex just isn't a big deal," Corrie says.

Perhaps the complicated mechanics of three-way sex has saved the trio from the passionate soul blending that proves so compelling to couples in the beginning and so problematic later on. For many women, nostalgia for their magical courtships only adds to the already considerable pressure to keep "doing it" long after the honeymoon is over. As a threesome, Corrie, Angela, and Skeeter had no such early memories to live up to. In addition, sex may not be a charged issue for the three women because they have nothing to prove. In contrast to twosomes, there is no hope that this trio will ever be eligible for mainstream membership.

Trying to envision sex that always included three partners was exactly what I needed to jostle some fixed notions that I was not even aware I had. Overall, talking to and writing about all these genital incidentalists has begun to reshape my clinical approach to lesbian bed death.

UNSEXING THE COUPLE

Every now and then I indulge in a Utopian dream of sex therapy. In my perfect world, both therapists and therapy-seeking clients realize that nonsexual pair-bonding is perfectly normal for many long-term lesbian couples. Friendships, Boston marriages, non-monogamy, collective living, intergenerational mixes, and even interspecies bonds are as highly valued as permanent, sexually-active partnerships. With the help of a therapist, no-longer-sexual mates meander among the profusion of alternative intimacies and, eventually choose the one that best suits their newly emerging circumstances and desires.

So far, few of my clients have shared my dream. And as long as traditional coupling remains the only visible and viable choice, I am faced with a daunting task: how to loosen the sex-couple connection at the very time couples are most desperate to tighten it.

When couples in the throes of a sexual crisis seek therapy, most sex therapists agree that the immediate goal is to remove the pressure. According to traditional sex therapists, the best way to provide immediate relief is simply to call a time-out from all explicitly sexual activity. Toward that end, therapists typically prescribe a regimen of nonsexual, sensually focused massages (Apfelbaum, Williams, & Greene, 1979). Such assignments are usually effective. Unfortunately, if this recess period goes on too long, partners get itchy to get on with the "real" work. In other words, genital sex, instead of being desanctified, has simply been put on hold.

I theorized that a more effective first step for embattled couples would be to cast some doubt on what actually constitutes sex. If partners couldn't be sure when they were or were not "doing it," they might be freer to experiment with other forms of intimacy—might, in fact, even dabble in genital incidentalism with each other.

In order to dissolve their certainty about sex, I assigned partners a series of are-we-or-aren't-we-doing-it exercises: these included playful massages that I hoped would scramble erotic and nonerotic zones and acts, and sex that started, rather than ended, with orgasms.

After some months of such mind-bending torment, one couple left in disgust. "We wanted," one partner said, "a sex life of abandon, and you wanted us to abandon our sex life." The other added, "I just wanted to be fixed. I didn't want a revolution." They had, they informed me, found a new therapist (Hall, 1991). When I bumped into the "no" half of the couple a year later, she had thrown in the towel on the relationship. "I fell in love," she said. "I found out that I'm really a bottom. I've found someone who can really top me."

It was easy to see why my efforts to deconstruct sex had backfired. When it came right down to it, I had no meaningful sex-substitutes to offer. And even if I could offer alternatives that would actually compete with sex, I could not marshal the cultural authority to legitimate them.

After a trip back to the drawing board, I decided to convert some of my personal consciousness-raising strategies into therapeutic techniques. Though not exactly paradigm shifting, my search for examples of alternative intimacies had given me more wiggle room when it came to sex. Perhaps it could do the same for my coupled clients.

It turned out that couples who came for sex therapy could conduct similar research without even leaving the office. We soon found that a thorough recounting of their own intimacy histories served the same purpose. For each of them, intimacy had meant different things at different times; their repertoires included devoted friendships, vulnerable confessions, passionate meltdowns, affectionate or playful touching, physical care-taking, intellectual sparring, orgasmic habits, and even the desperate intensity of lovers who sense an impending breakup.

The definitional boundaries of intimacy expanded even further as we looked at the ways the sexual dynamics between partners had become a stand-in for early family dramas. When it seemed pertinent, I threw in the variations I had come across: the minimalist sex that seemed so characteristic of long-term lesbian partners and the recently discovered three-way genital incidentalism.

There were plenty of slip-ups during this process. For example, I frequently found myself secretly rooting for the more conventional partner, that is, the one whose desires, by mainstream standards, seemed perfectly "normal." But when I caught myself in such a collusion, I guessed that the partners may also have gotten mired, without knowing it, in the conviction that the partner who wanted sex was superior to the other. Making these pass/fail dynamics explicit helped us appreciate the plurality of possible intimacies, as well as how very distinct partners' individual maps were.

At first I thought that this mapmaking would lead to a collaboration on mutually-expanded and inclusive maps. I hoped that partners, after listening to one another, could come up with a new combination of playfulness and sensation that would be meaningful to both of them. Occasionally, a reinvention of intimacy has occurred. But mostly, after going through paroxysms of despair about seemingly irreconcilable differences, partners have come back reporting slightly improved versions of their customary sexual contact. Even though there are plenty of ups and downs, with no quantum leaps into genital incidentalism, I do sense some subtle loosening of the sex-couple connection.

This approach has not worked with all couples. For some, careful attention to their histories and reactions only seems to buttress their adversarial positions and impasses. Most of these couples drop out of therapy quickly. More challenging are the ones who stay when nothing positive seems to be happening. But I suppose that is not surprising. Rather than give up the whole category of sex, and their lesbian identities along with it, lesbian couples will find new techniques, new roles, new therapists, new lovers, or will simply continue to search for new insights to explain the absence of sex in their lives. And by continuing to participate in such searches, I wonder if I am reinforcing couples' convictions that their identities as lesbians and as couples hinge on their sexual performance.

On the other hand, ongoing sex therapy, itself, may be a useful substitute for sex. Even though partners are not actually "doing it," they may be getting some of the relationship witnessing and validation that is missing outside the session. By spending an hour every week with a guide gingerly exploring the private and public meanings of couple intimacy, partners may satisfy, at least symbolically, the imperative to have sex regularly. And perhaps the lesbian therapist and the lesbian couple, as they continue to probe and peek, form a voyeuristic threesome of sorts. At first glance, such an approach flies in the face of the systems theorists' warnings about boundary violations (Schultz, 1984). Yet, unless therapists somehow challenge the definitional boundary that surrounds sex, clients and therapists alike will continue to be subject to the tyrannies of "doing it."

Unique sexual problems require unorthodox solutions. The more I-don't-knows and in-betweens that sex therapists' and their lesbian clients can generate, the less they will feel exiled by mainstream norms. It is, after all, almost impossible to marginalize someone who already feels perfectly at home in the margins.

REFERENCES

Apfelbaum, B., Williams, M., & Greene, S. (1979). BSTG couple sex therapy assignments. In *Expanding the boundaries of sex therapy: Selected papers of the Berkeley Sex Therapy Group*. Self-published in Berkeley, CA.

Blumstein, P., & Schwartz, P. (1983). *American couples*. New York: William Morrow.

Brain, R. (1976). *Friends and lovers*. New York: Basic Books.

Cline, S. (1993). *Women, celibacy and passion*. London: Optima.

Hall, M. (1991). Ex-Therapy to sex therapy: Notes from the margins. In C. Silverstein (Ed.), *Gays, lesbians, and their therapists* (pp. 84-97). New York: Norton.

Hall, M. (1993). "Why limit me to ecstasy?" Toward a positive model of genital incidentalism among friends and other lovers. In E. Rothblum & K. Brehony (Eds.), *Boston marriages: Romantic but asexual relationships among contemporary lesbians* (pp. 41-61). Amherst: University of Massachusetts Press.

Hall, M. (1995). Clit notes. In K. Jay (Ed.), *Dyke life: From growing up to growing old, a celebration of the lesbian experience* (pp. 195-215). New York: Basic Books.

Huston, M., & Schwartz, P. (1995). The relationships of lesbians and gay men. In J. Wood & S. Duck (Eds.), *Understudied relationships: Off the beaten path* (pp. 89-121). Thousand Oaks, CA: Sage.

Laing, R. (1970). *The divided self*. New York: Pantheon.

Lever, J. Lesbian Sex Survey. *The Advocate*, 8/22/95 (pp. 22-30).

Raymond, J. (1986). *A Passion for friends: Toward a philosophy of female affection*. Boston: Beacon.

Schultz, S. (1984). *Family systems therapy: An integration*. New York: Jason Aronson.

Wecks, G., & Hof, L. (1987). *Integrating sex and marital therapy*. New York: Brunner/Mazel.

Cultural Considerations
in Couples Therapy

Pamela A. Hays

SUMMARY. This paper offers a framework for considering cultural influences in couples therapy. Emphasis is placed on the therapist's responsibility to engage in an ongoing self-assessment of personal biases, areas of inexperience, and privilege. With a focus on couples of ethnic minority cultures, suggestions are offered for establishing rapport, understanding values, and appreciating strengths. *[Article copies available for a fee from The Haworth Document Delivery Service: 1-800-342-9678. E-mail address: getinfo@haworth.com]*

While family systems and feminist therapies have raised awareness of the need to consider an individual's social context, both of these fields have until recently paid little attention to the contexts of people of color (Brown, 1994; Brown & Root, 1990; McGoldrick, Pearce, & Giordano, 1982). The purpose of this paper is to encourage therapists to consider cultural influences in their work with

---

Pamela Hays received her MS in counseling psychology from the University of Alaska and PhD in clinical psychology from the University of Hawaii. Since 1989, she has worked as a core faculty member in the Graduate Psychology Program at Antioch University Seattle.

The author would like to thank Peg LeVine and Jawed Zouari for their helpful suggestions regarding this paper.

Address correspondence to: Pam Hays, Graduate Psychology Program, Antioch University, 2607 Second Avenue, Seattle, WA 98121-1211.

[Haworth co-indexing entry note]: "Cultural Considerations in Couples Therapy." Hays, Pamela A. Co-published simultaneously in *Women & Therapy* (The Haworth Press, Inc.) Vol. 19, No. 3, 1996, pp. 13-23; and: *Couples Therapy: Feminist Perspectives* (ed: Marcia Hill and Esther D. Rothblum) The Haworth Press, Inc., 1996, pp. 13-23; and: *Couples Therapy: Feminist Perspectives* (ed: Marcia Hill and Esther D. Rothblum) Harrington Park Press, an imprint of The Haworth Press, Inc., 1996, pp. 13-23. Single or multiple copies of this article are available for a fee from The Haworth Document Delivery Service [1-800-342-9678, 9:00 a.m. - 5:00 p.m. (EST). E-mail address: getinfo@haworth.com].

diverse couples. A framework is described for considering cultural (including gender-related) influences on both clients and therapists. The importance of personal work aimed at challenging one's own biases is discussed. And with a focus on couples of ethnic minority cultures, suggestions are offered for establishing rapport, understanding values, and appreciating strengths.

BECOMING MORE CULTURALLY RESPONSIVE

In recognition of the needs of minority cultures and groups traditionally excluded from psychological research and practice, the American Psychological Association (1993) recently published the "Guidelines for Providers of Psychological Services to Ethnic, Linguistic, and Culturally Diverse Populations." The American Counseling Association's Division of Multicultural Counseling and Development has published a similar set of "Multicultural Counseling Competencies and Standards" for counselors (Sue, Arrendondo, & McDavis, 1992). A helpful way to organize the influences described in these documents is via the acronym "ADDRESSING" which reminds therapists to consider the following in their work: *A*ge and generational influences, *D*evelopmental and acquired *D*isability, *R*eligion, *E*thnicity, *S*ocial status, *S*exual orientation, *I*ndigenous heritage, *N*ational origin, and *G*ender (Hays & LeVine, in press). Corresponding to each of these influences are a number of minority cultures and groups which have been neglected, marginalized or considered in a biased way in mainstream psychotherapy research, namely, older people; people with disabilities; people of religious, ethnic, and national minority cultures; people of Indigenous or Aboriginal heritage (i.e., Native Alaskans, Native Hawaiians, and American Indians in the U.S., and First Nations people in Canada—see Note 1); people of lower social status or class by education, income, occupation; rural or urban origin; people who are gay, lesbian, and bisexual; and women (Hays, 1995).

The first step towards becoming a culturally responsive therapist involves the assessment of one's own areas of bias, ignorance and inexperience. This work is best conceptualized as a life-long process, with its success dependent on the degree of commitment held by the therapist. Assuming that the therapist holds such a commitment, the ADDRESSING acronym can be used as a beginning guide for exploring the impact of cultural influences on the therapist's worldview (i.e., the impact of *age* and generational influences, and experience or inexperience with elders; personal experience or inexperience with *disability* and/or people who have disabilities, and so on), (see Hays, in press, for greater detail). Concomitantly, through a consideration of the privileges one receives as a member of dominant groups related to each of the ADDRESSING categories, the therapist may become more aware of the limits of her or his awareness and experience.

For example, consider K, a 35-year-old Euroamerican, lesbian therapist. K considers her awareness of minority groups and social inequities to be high because through her personal experiences, academic training, and social interactions, she has developed a solid knowledge of the impact of sexism and heterosexism on many women. However, if K were to consider her knowledge and experience in relation to privileged groups in each of the ADDRESSING categories, she would find that much of her learning has been limited to people of cultural identities similar to her own. That is, beginning with *age* and generational influences, K's experiences are limited to young and middle-aged women. With regard to *disability,* she has no close friends who have disabilities, and has no experience with disability herself. While she identifies her *religious* beliefs as secular, she benefits from the privileges of a Christian upbringing, and has no close relationships with people who are Muslim, Jewish, Hindu or Buddhist. Similarly, the people in her closest circle are, like her, of Euroamerican *ethnicities.* And her academic training has primarily been with and about non-disabled, young to middle-aged women of White middle-class *social status.*

Focusing on K's areas of privilege does not negate the heightened awareness, knowledge or experiences she holds in relation to gender and sexual orientation. However, it does call attention to the limits of this knowledge and experience. Moreover, by exploring the knowledge gaps created by these privileges, K could be challenged to move beyond her own experience and become engaged with people with whom she does not currently identify.

The more knowledgeable a therapist is about clients' cultural contexts, the closer her hypotheses and questions will be to clients' experiences and situations. Returning to the same example, consider K's ability to work with a young, college-educated, Euroamerican lesbian couple who present their problem as "difficulty resolving arguments." In this case, K's training and personal experience have given her the awareness, background knowledge, and comfort level to ask appropriate questions, make reasonable hypotheses, and respond sensitively to both partners. In contrast, imagine K with an older, African American couple who are seeking couples therapy following the husband's stroke. Neither K's training nor her personal relationships have included African Americans, people with disabilities, or older couples. As a result, her hypotheses with this second couple would be less accurate and her questions farther off the mark. Furthermore, she would be more likely to unintentionally offend the couple by her lack of culture-specific knowledge. For example, her use of first names with an older African American couple might be intended as friendliness but be perceived as disrespectful (Hines & Boyd-Franklin, 1982).

While the ADDRESSING framework is no substitute for culture-specific knowledge, it does draw the therapist's attention to those areas in which she lacks information and/or experience, in relation to specific clients. It can also be used to remind the therapist of the diversity *within* ethnic minority cultures as a result of differences related to each of the ADDRESSING factors (age, disability, religion, etc.). This "diversity within" orientation avoids unidimensional conceptualizations of identity, and thus works against the tendency to make inaccurate assumptions about clients based on physical appearances. Given the large number of people who identify with more than one minority culture (e.g., women of color, older lesbian women, gay men of color, women with disabilities), the acknowledgement and consideration of bicultural and multicultural identities is essential (see Boden, 1992; Comas-Diaz & Greene, 1994; Gutiérrez & Dworkin, 1992; Root, 1992; Schoonmaker, 1993).

Establishing Rapport

Because the therapist holds power as a result of her professional education, occupation and role, clients will often assume that she holds the same biases as the dominant culture. This is especially true when the therapist is a member of a dominant cultural group to which the couple does not belong (whether by ethnicity, gender, religion, or any of the ADDRESSING factors). To counter this power imbalance, it can be helpful at the beginning of a session to engage in some socially-oriented conversation in which the therapist discloses personal information, too. This personalized communication allows *clients* the opportunity to assess the *therapist*'s awareness and ability to understand them (Hays, 1996-b). It is also responsive to the cultural preferences of many people, for example, in expectations of *personalismo* among many Latino and Latina people (Morales, 1992), a desire for "mutuality" in relationships among many older women (Greenberg & Motenko, 1994), concern with respect and reciprocity among many American Indian people (Matheson, 1986), and an interest in making a "person-to-person connection" among many Black families (Boyd-Franklin, 1989).

To ensure that both partners in a couple are able to use the language in which they feel most comfortable, referral to a bilingual therapist or the inclusion of an interpreter may be necessary. Although one member of a couple may be bilingual and capable of interpreting, s/he should never be asked to take on this role because such an arrangement places her or him in a conflictual position (Ho, 1987).

Understanding Values

Dominant cultural values permeate the profession of psychology to such an extent that they are often invisible to therapists of diverse identities. For example, Tamura and Lau (1992) describe the case of a Japanese couple living in England with their 10-year-old daughter, who were seen by a Japanese therapist (Tamura) and a supervisory team of British therapists. The wife spoke little English, was socially isolated at home and becoming increasingly depressed, while her daughter attended school all day and her husband worked long hours. The British therapists working with this couple framed the problem as a "dilemma of choice" (suggesting that the husband seemed to have two marriages, one with his wife and one with his work). The husband and wife rejected this interpretation, stating that they did not consider his work commitment a matter of choice. Acknowledging the normality of this attitude in Japan, the Japanese therapist accepted the husband's commitment to his work as a given, and framed the problem as one of inadequate social support for the wife (noting that support from family members and other women would have been available to her in Japan). This latter view emphasized integration over the British focus on differentiation. Interestingly, the intervention still focused on helping the couple to provide more effective emotional support for one another, but the latter frame was more acceptable to the couple because it fit their value system.

The emphasis on differentiation and individualism in family systems research reflects the dominance of values rooted in middle-class, patriarchal, European Christian culture in the U.S. (herein referred to as Euroamerican). These influences may be easily overlooked by therapists who have been educated in a curriculum designed by and for Euroamericans. To counteract the "cultural encapsulation" inherent to this profession (a term used by Wrenn, 1962), ongoing personal work outside the therapy setting is essential, as are consultation with cultural liaisons and culturally diverse professionals.

Value conflicts can also arise *within* the familial system of a couple, particularly when partners are of different cultures. (Interracial marriages in the U.S. number at least one million [Thornton, 1992], which is a conservative estimate of intercultural couples given the additional number of unmarried heterosexual, gay and lesbian couples.) For example, consider the situation of a middle-class, married, intercultural couple in their early 50s. Mrs. A is Euroamerican, secular in her religious beliefs (although reared as a Presbyterian), and has recently begun working outside the home after the couple's last child left for college. Mr. A is an Arab American man who immigrated to the U.S. as a teenager with his family; he identifies himself as Palestinian and Muslim, although he does not practice his religion. Following the death of his father in Jordan, Mr. A assumed that his mother would come to live with them in the U.S., but Mrs. A preferred to find her mother-in-law a nearby apartment or retirement home. Mr. A considered this suggestion to be irresponsible and uncaring, while Mrs. A believed that it would be more likely to maintain their relationships because each person would be assured of their independence.

In this case, Mrs. A's viewpoint corresponds to the dominant Euroamerican cultural concern with individualism and personal independence. In contrast, Mr. A's perspective reflects values common among many Arab and Muslim cultures, namely, responsibility for one's family, concern with social support and physical proximity in relationships (El-Islam, 1982; Hays & Zouari, 1995). This is not to say that Mrs. A cares less for her family, or that Mr. A is unconcerned with maintaining his own independence; rather, the difference is primarily one of emphasis, in what is given more weight.

Acknowledging differences in values is the first step towards addressing them. As McGoldrick and Preto (1984) note, differences can create conflict, but "the opposite problem, failing to appreciate differences that are rooted in ethnicity" can be equally difficult (p. 348). With Mr. and Mrs. A, the danger for the therapist would be in the automatic acceptance of the dominant cultural perspective (represented by Mrs. A), because it is so subtly reinforced by mainstream systems theories. Instead, a more balanced approach would involve helping the couple to explore the influence of cultural beliefs (and person-specific experiences) on their values and the relationship of these values to their individual viewpoints. This understanding might lead the couple to consider ways in which their values could be changed or modified, thus creating the possibility of new solutions and/or a compromise. For example, Mr. and Mrs. A might decide upon an arrangement in which Mr. A's mother lives with the couple (a response to Mr. A's values), but with the agreement that specific steps be taken to ensure a comfortable level of independence for Mrs. A and the couple. These steps might include Mr. A's acceptance of primary responsibility for taking his mother to the doctor's and shopping, the agreement that Mrs. A would continue to work outside the home, and a commitment to taking weekend vacations as a couple on a regular basis.

Appreciating Strengths

Psychological theories, diagnostic systems, and tests of intelligence, personality and behavior have routinely assumed Euroamerican culture to be the standard against which all other people are compared. Not surprisingly, people of ethnic minority cultures, people who speak English as a second language, gay and lesbian people, older people, people with disabilities, and women have traditionally been found deficient or abnormal in relation to the Euroamerican ideal. Combined with psychology's focus on pathology, this negative orientation has meant that therapists tend to recognize problems more readily than they perceive strengths in clients of minority cultures and groups (Stevenson & Renard, 1993).

To counteract this tendency to see differences as deficiencies, Kim (1985) recommends reframing clients' behaviors in ways which validate their culture-specific uses. For example, with Asian American families, Kim reframes what a Eurocentric therapist might call "resistance" as a normal desire to protect one's family. With families who show a strong need for confidentiality, he points out (to the family) the strength they possess, as evident in their willingness to seek help despite strong cultural biases against doing so.

Similarly, in her work with low-income Black and White families, Westbrooks (1995) found that many of the characteristics judged dysfunctional from a dominant systems perspective were functional and even constructive in the contexts of these families' lives. For example, the Eurocentric assumption that communication should be "open and direct" was contradicted by some low-income families' belief that "communication involves a time to speak and a time to be silent." And the idea that family values need to be consistent with the broader cultural context was countered by a healthy suspicion of the larger society as "a potential threat to healthy family values" (p. 141).

Examples of other culturally-related strengths and supports which may not be immediately apparent to therapists include cultural networks; extended family relationships (including non-blood related relatives); religious faith and supportive religious communities; beliefs or attitudes which help a person cope with obstacles; traditional celebrations, rituals, and artistic/recreational pursuits (e.g., women's sewing and embroidery groups, and for men in some traditional cultures, fishing); a strong connection to the land and natural environment; and participation in political or social activist groups. It is also important to recognize the strengths of bicultural and multicultural couples who have successfully resolved the tensions related to their own diversity; these intercultural relationships offer opportunities for interpersonal connections, new patterns of behavior, and creative solutions which might otherwise be unavailable to each partner alone (Falicov, 1995; McGoldrick & Preto, 1984).

CONCLUSION

This article has described a broad framework for considering the impact on therapists and couples of diverse cultural influences including *A*ge and generational influences, *D*evelopmental and acquired *D*isability, *R*eligion, *E*thnicity, *S*ocial status, *S*exual orientation, *I*ndigenous heritage, *N*ational origin, and *G*ender (which form the ADDRESSING acronym). With a focus on couples of ethnic minority cultures, suggestions were provided for establishing rapport, understanding values, and appreciating strengths. Finally, emphasis was placed on the need for therapists to hold a strong commitment to learning more about and from people of diverse minority cultures and groups.

NOTE

1. In the U.S., the term "ethnic minority" is used in reference to (and by) many ethnic groups which have been marginalized by the dominant Euroamerican culture, including people of Indigenous heritage (i.e., American Indians, Native Alaskans, and Native Hawaiians). However, in Canada, the term is used primarily in reference to non-Anglo and non-French *immigrant* groups; the original (or Aboriginal) people of Canada refer to themselves as the First Nations. In recognition of these different perspectives, the ADDRESSING acronym includes both *I*ndigenous heritage and *E*thnicity.

REFERENCES

American Psychological Association. (1993). Guidelines for providers of psychological services to ethnic, linguistic, and culturally diverse populations. *American Psychologist, 48,* 45-48.

Boden, R. (1992). Psychotherapy with physically disabled lesbians. In S. H. Dworkin & F. J. Gutiérrez (Eds.), *Counseling gay men and lesbians: Journey to the end of the rainbow* (pp. 157-174). Alexandria, VA: American Counseling Association.

Boyd-Franklin, N. (1989). *Black families in therapy: A multisystems approach.* New York: Guilford Press.

Brown, L. (1994). *Subversive dialogues: Theory in feminist therapy.* New York: Basic Books.

Brown, L., & Root, M. P. P. (Eds.) (1990). *Diversity and complexity in feminist therapy.* New York: Harrington Park Press.

Comaz-Diaz, L., & Greene, B. (Eds.) (1994). *Women of color: Integrating ethnic and gender identites in psychotherapy.* New York: Guilford Press.

El-Islam, M. F. (1982). Arabic cultural psychiatry. *Transcultural Psychiatric Research Review, 19,* 5-23.

Falicov, C. (1995). Cross-cultural marriages. In N. S. Jacobsen & A. S. Gurman (Eds.), *Clinical handbook of couple therapy* (pp. 231-246). New York: Guilford Press.

Greenberg, S., & Motenko, A. K. (1994). Women growing older: Partnerships for change. In M. P. Mirken (Ed.), *Women in context* (pp. 96-117). New York: Guilford Press.

Gutiérrez, F. J., & Dworkin, S. H. (1992). Gay, lesbian, and African American: Managing the integration of identities. In S. H. Dworkin & F. J. Gutiérrez (Eds.), *Counseling gay men and lesbians: Journey to the end of the rainbow* (pp. 141-156). Alexandria, VA: American Counseling Association.

Hays, P. A. (1996). Addressing the complexities of culture and gender in counseling. *Journal of Counseling and Development, 74,* 332-338.

Hays, P. A. (1996). Culturally responsive assessment with diverse older clients. *Professional Psychology: Research and Practice, 27,* 188-193.

Hays. P. A., & LeVine, P. (in press). *Culturally responsive assessment and diagnosis.* New York: Guilford Press.

Hays, P. A., & Zouari, J. (1995). Social change, stress, and mental health among rural, village and urban Tunisian women. *International Journal of Psychology, 30*(1), 69-90.

Hines, P. M., & Boyd-Franklin, N. (1982). Black families. In M. McGoldrick, J. K. Pearce, & J. Giordano (Eds.), *Ethnicity and family therapy* (pp. 84-107). New York: Guilford Press.

Ho, Man Keung. (1987). *Family therapy with ethnic minorities.* Newbury Park, CA: Sage.

Kim, S. C. (1985). Family therapy for Asian Americans: A strategic structural framework. *Psychotherapy, 22,* 342-348.

Matheson, L. (1986). If you are not an Indian, how do you treat an Indian? In H. P. Lefley & P. B. Pedersen, *Cross-cultural training for mental health professionals* (pp. 115-130). Springfield, IL: Charles C Thomas.

McGoldrick, M., Pearce, J. K., & Giordano, J. (Eds.) (1982). *Ethnicity and family therapy.* New York: Guilford Press.

McGoldrick, M., & Preto, N. G. (1984). Ethnic intermarriage: Implications for therapy. *Family Process, 23,* 347-364.

Morales, E. S. (1992). Counseling Latino Gays and Latina lesbians. In S. H. Dworkin & F. J. Gutiérrez (Eds.), *Counseling gay men and lesbians: Journey to the end of the rainbow* (pp. 125-140). Alexandria, VA: American Counseling Association.

Root, M. (Ed.) (1992). *Racially mixed people in America* (pp. 64-76). Newbury Park, CA: Sage.

Schoonmaker, C. (1993). Aging lesbians: Bearing the burden of triple shame. *Women & Therapy, 14,* 21-31.

Stevenson, H. C., & Renard, G. (1993). Trusting wise old owls: Therapeutic use of cultural strengths in African American families. *Professional Psychology: Research and Practice, 24,* 433-442.

Sue, D. W., Arredondo, P., & McDavis, R. J. (1992). Multicultural counseling competencies and standards: A call to the profession. *Journal of Multicultural Counseling & Development, 20,* 64-88.

Tamura, T., & Lau, A. (1992). Connectedness versus separateness: Applicability of family therapy to Japanese families. *Family Process, 31,* 319-340.

Thornton, M. C. (1992). The quiet immigration: Foreign spouses of U.S. citizens, 1945-1985. In M. Root (Ed.), *Racially mixed people in America* (pp. 64-76). Newbury Park, CA: Sage.

Westbrooks, K. L. (1995). *Functional low-income families: Activating strengths.* New York: Vantage Press.

Wrenn, G. C. (1962). The culturally encapsulated counselor. *Harvard Educational Review, 32,* 444-449.

Loving Across Race and Class Divides: Relational Challenges and the Interracial Lesbian Couple

Sarah F. Pearlman

SUMMARY. Similar to their heterosexual counterparts, lesbians are increasingly meeting and falling in love with women very different than themselves — differences which include race and class and thus, cultural background. Yet, there are distinct challenges which confront the interracial lesbian couple such as homophobia, racism, and limited social support from family and friends as illustrated through the narratives of two composite couples. A race, class, and culture sensitive psychotherapy is recommended. This enables clinicians to articulate perspectives which reframe and "unpersonalize" power struggles and disclose cultural differences in values and meanings as well as affirm those special joys and rewards when attraction and intimacy are joined to cultural difference. *[Article copies available for a fee from The Haworth Document Delivery Service: 1-800-342-9678. E-mail address: getinfo@haworth.com]*

Sarah F. Pearlman is Assistant Professor in the Doctoral Program in Clinical Psychology at the University of Hartford and is a licensed psychologist in private practice in Hartford. She is an editor and author of articles in the anthology, *Lesbian Psychologies: Explorations and Challenges* as well as other articles on lesbian relationships.

Address correspondence to: Sarah F. Pearlman, PsyD, Doctoral Program in Clinical Psychology, University of Hartford, West Hartford, CT 06117.

[Haworth co-indexing entry note]: "Loving Across Race and Class Divides: Relational Challenges and the Interracial Lesbian Couple." Pearlman, Sarah F. Co-published simultaneously in *Women & Therapy* (The Haworth Press, Inc.) Vol. 19, No. 3, 1996, pp. 25-35; and: *Couples Therapy: Feminist Perspectives* (ed: Marcia Hill and Esther D. Rothblum) The Haworth Press, Inc., 1996, pp. 25-35; and: *Couples Therapy: Feminist Perspectives* (ed: Marcia Hill and Esther D. Rothblum) Harrington Park Press, an imprint of The Haworth Press, Inc., 1996, pp. 25-35. Single or multiple copies of this article are available for a fee from The Haworth Document Delivery Service [1-800-342-9678, 9:00 a.m. - 5:00 p.m. (EST). E-mail address: getinfo@haworth.com].

No one ever told us we had to study our lives, make of our lives a study . . .

—Adrienne Rich (1978, p. 73)

Although there are now a variety of books and articles available on the unique relational dynamics and particular stressors which impact lover relationships between women (Burch, 1993, 1987; Kresten & Bepko, 1980; Pearlman, 1989; Varga, 1987), most of the psychological literature has focused on the experience of Caucasian or Euro-American women, and lesbian couples of color as well as mixed-race lesbian couples have received little attention. Yet, similar to their heterosexual counterparts (Burnette, 1995), lesbians are increasingly meeting, becoming attracted to, falling in love, and establishing romantic relationships with women who are very different than themselves–differences which include race and ethnicity as well as class-of-origin or current socioeconomic status. However, although there are many similarities between mixed-race heterosexual and lesbian couples, the interracial heterosexual couple does not have to manage homophobia which further compounds family acceptance and limits social support. In addition, male privilege and gender based social rules do offer familiar relational patterns and roles.

It is crucial to understand that one's race and class background constitute one's cultural origins in that both race and class are primary determinants of culture and cultural difference. Also, race, more often than not, can determine both class background and later socioeconomic status. Thus, clinicians who work both individually and in couples therapy with lesbians who are in interracial relationships are challenged to be both race and class sensitive as well as knowledgeable about diverse cultures. Although individual dynamics and couple struggles connected to those issues should remain in focus, it is imperative that clinicians also attend to different norms, values, and meanings such as obligations to immediate and extended families; patterns and values regarding money, time, and leisure; interpersonal or interactional styles; styles of mothering and child-rearing; sources of self-esteem and sense of self; and differing levels of access to privilege and power.

Clinicians have their own pictures of and belief systems about interracial relationships such as that selection of a Caucasian woman means lingering internalized racism or that choice of a minority partner suggests low self-esteem and need to feel superior as well as sexual objectification or erotization of the "other" (Kadi, 1993). While these factors can play some role, there are always multiple motivations beneath behaviors and preferences. That is, there are both underlying conscious as well as unconscious meanings and dynamics which shape the selection of any significant relationship (uniracial or interracial). However, these do not exclude other factors such as genuine liking, respect, and enjoyment in addition to sexual attraction which constitute the strengths of many interracial relationships.

The point is that clinicians, and perhaps Caucasian middle-class clinicans in particular, who work with lesbians joined in interracial relationships, must struggle with another kind of countertransference. This means monitoring awareness of one's own racism or racist views and feelings, one's attitudes towards class, and one's feelings, assumptions, and personal/psychological beliefs about people who enter into interracial unions as well as identifications and counter-identifications with each woman in the mixed-race/mixed-class couple.

COMPOSITE COUPLE I: JULIA AND SUSAN

Julia is a forty-five year old Puerto Rican born woman who immigrated with her family to the United States at age nine. Her partner of six years, Susan, is a fifty-year old Caucasian woman of English, Irish, and German descent. Julia's formal education included some business courses following high school and she now works in an accounting firm. Susan completed four years of college and is a graphic artist.

While it was Susan who first suggested couples therapy, Julia, although initially reluctant, eventually agreed. Both women stated that arguments were becoming more frequent and they feared that unless they could resolve some important issues, their relationship "would come apart at the seams." Each woman has been previously married and has adult children. Susan's two children are now married and live in a nearby state. Julia's one child, a son, is living with his girlfriend.

Julia and Susan described their relationship as very satisfying until around two years ago, a year which they characterized as full of multiple crises including a car accident, hospitalization, and the death of a sibling. This was also the year that Julia's son moved into his own apartment so that they were able to live together as a couple for the first time.

Exploration of the prevalent couple differences and conflicts included Julia's difficulty with a friendship between Susan and an ex-lover. Susan thought that Julia was too possessive and jealous and was angry that she did not trust her. Julia admitted to jealousy, but found the relationship threatening and did not think that friendships with other women should be so important. Her friends and social companions were her family members and time separate from Susan was spent with her mother and sisters or visits to her son and girlfriend.

Much of therapy followed the usual course of questioning and clarification as I learned about Julia's and Susan's families of origin, their growing up and marital history, their coming out and prior relationships, couple history and family reactions, their sexual relationship, adjustments to living together, and prevalent sources of conflict. While there were multiple factors which were affecting Julia's and Susan's relationship, their major source of conflict was Susan's view of Julia's relationship with her family, especially her son. To Susan, Julia was overinvolved with both her family and her son who Susan described as a spoiled and overly indulged young man. Unlike Susan's children, Julia's son had never accepted that his mother was a lesbian. He refused to visit their home unless Susan was absent and made it clear that he did not want to be around her.

While his negation of their relationship infuriated her, Susan was more hurt that Julia did not "put him in his place" and felt that her partner was choosing her son over her. Julia, however, believed that her son needed more time and would eventually come around, and expressed fears that she might lose him as well as relationships with future grandchildren if she spoke up and confronted his behavior. Julia and Susan also had very different communication styles.

While Susan could be direct and confrontative, Julia would hold back feelings until moved by anger and then would explode.

As the conversation turned towards cultural styles of family relationships and mothering, Susan was able to identify patterns and values from her own background and family/cultural heritage. She had grown up in a financially secure, middle class family (both parents were high school teachers) characterized by emphasis on formality and politeness between family members. She, like her parents, believed that children should be brought up to be independent and that parents should not intrude or interfere in their adult children's lives. Although she felt emotionally close to both her daughters, contact between them was mostly limited to birthdays and holidays.

Julia had a very different background. Her parents had separated before leaving Puerto Rico and her family was dependent upon public assistance during most of her growing up years. Julia was close to and had frequent contact with both immediate and extended family members who were all very involved in each other's lives. Julia stated that she enjoyed "indulging" her son through gifts of money and food and it was apparent that her sense of self and self-esteem were very connected to motherhood, close family relationships, and family obligations which, at times, included financial assistance.

Susan, however, was uncomfortable in the presence of Julia's family and indicated that she felt unsafe as a white person in their neighborhood. She stated also that their homes were noisy and crowded with no privacy, and that everyone would often speak Spanish which she did not understand. Julia's response was that Susan was saying her family was not as good as hers and, in turn, would call Susan's parents' home "the morgue."

Julia's picture of the relationship she wanted with Susan was that of a marriage, that is, couple and family centered. Susan's picture, however, included friendships with other lesbian couples as well as activities and friendships of her own. While they did have lesbian couple friends, all were Caucasian and the social events and activities they participated in were attended primarily by Caucasian women. While Julia stated that she did enjoy these activities, she was intimidated at times, and expressed that she often felt self-conscious of her accented speech and that she spoke "badly." She believed that she was not as educated or articulate as many of the white women, that they would not be interested in what she had to say, and that she was more private about family matters which seemed to be a common subject of conversation. She wished that she could meet other Puerto Rican lesbians who were like herself (similar income level and values) and available for friendship.

While psychotherapy with this couple focused on many aspects of their relationship, it was the exploration and recognition of the cultural meanings of their behaviors, values, and patterns which allowed Julia and Susan to "unpersonalize" their conflicts. To accomplish this, Susan needed to understand that she, too, as a white person, was part of a culture which had shaped her behaviors and values, including child-rearing, expectations of adult children, and her picture of significant relationships. Thus, individual mothering and family relationship values became addressed in a cultural context so that power struggle dynamics resulting in defensiveness and anger decreased and a new kind of conversation was able to take place.

Therapy terminated when communication improved sufficiently so that Julia and Susan were able to negotiate and compromise more effectively. For example, Susan asked Julia to inform her about visiting times and holiday plans with her son and other family members. She also asked that they have "couple time" following Julia's visits to her son, suggesting that she drop her off and pick her up as a way of affirming their relationship. In turn, Julia requested that Susan tell her before she made plans with her ex-lover, that she try to become more involved with her family and perhaps learn to speak a little Spanish.

COMPOSITE COUPLE II: SHERYL AND GENA

Sheryl is an African American woman of forty-two and works as a nursing supervisor in a city hospital. Gena is fifty-three years old, Jewish, and teaches in a community college. They have been in a relationship for seven years and have lived together for the past three years. Both women have been married and each has two adult children.

Sheryl and Gena agreed to try couple therapy with hopes that a third person could help them make an important decision. They had been discussing the possibility of living separately, but feared they would not be able to maintain their relationship if they resided in separate households. Both women stated that although living together had many rewards, money and the sharing of expenses had always been a difficult issue. Fighting was becoming more "nasty" and they each had little hope that their relationship problems could be resolved.

To Sheryl, Gena was overly concerned and inflexible about money matters. To Gena, Sheryl constantly mismanaged money and although their respective incomes were comparable, Sheryl was often without money so that Gena had to assume responsibility for their living expenses. In addition, both women described very different time and planning styles. Gena tended to plan activities in advance, which Sheryl felt put her at the mercy of her schedule and appointment book. Gena stated that Sheryl would often decide what she wanted to do at the last minute and would change plans without consulting her.

Sheryl and Gena had very different backgrounds. Sheryl grew up in a large family (three sisters, two brothers) in a city housing project. She described both parents as very hardworking (her father was a painter; her mother, a nurse's aide), but that financial survival had always been a struggle. Sheryl was also the one member of her family to attend and graduate from college and is viewed as the most successful child. She describes herself as very different from other family members in that she is the person who has most assimilated to the majority or white culture. She attributes this to her education, her work situation, and the opportunity through social exposure to meet white women as a lesbian.

Gena grew up in a white collar, Jewish family. Both parents were the children of Russian immigrants and she described her early home life as characterized by unhappiness, conflict, and frequent arguments between her mother and father. Thus, fighting with Sheryl was experienced as a painful repetition.

Although the initial presenting problem focused on conflicts over money, Sheryl and Gena described many other stressors. They were very isolated as a couple and had few social supports. Both their families of origin had many adjustments in accepting their lesbianism as well as their racial difference and neither woman felt comfortable with the other's family. Thus, closeness with family members was maintained as individuals rather than as a couple. In addition, Gena stated that her friends had never taken their relationship seriously and believed that she would eventually lose interest in Sheryl. Sheryl indicated that she felt uncomfortable, angry, and intimidated by Gena's friends, and that she did not enjoy their "talk" parties. However, Sheryl also stated that her own friends put her down for being with a white woman and would encourage her to date African American lesbians. Both sets of friends tended to support breaking up rather than resolution of problems.

Sheryl's and Gena's values on mothering were similar and it was important to both women that they remain close to their children. However, the nature of their obligations to children and family members was very different. While Gena would help her children financially at times, Sheryl's children as well as brothers and sisters were often in need of money and would ask her to help them out. To Sheryl, Gena's family was well off and didn't need money while hers was poor and that she had no choice but to help out, even if it "kept her poor."

Thus, Sheryl was often without sufficient money to pay her share of expenses nor did she have money enough for leisure activities such as travel vacations which were important to Gena. Gena then would pay Sheryl's way, although angry and resentful. To Sheryl, relationships meant partners pooling money and helping each other out depending on need. Gena's picture of a relationship was that of equal financial responsibility, adding that Sheryl's intentions were moot because she would never have any money. In addition, Gena was very critical of Sheryl's spending patterns and said that Sheryl spent too much on clothes and lottery tickets. Sheryl's reply was that lottery tickets were her concern, that it was important for her "to look good," and that if Gena didn't want to, it was her business.

Therapy gave this couple the space to talk about these problems and to understand that some of their conflicts such as values and patterns about money as well as the immediate present-versus-future orientation and planning were connected to class-of-origin differences. In addition, Sheryl's opinions of Gena's concern with money were interpreted by Gena as having meanings of anti-Semitism and Jewish stereotypes. Sheryl, in turn, heard Gena's criticisms as putting her down for being stupid, indicating racial prejudice and disrespect. However, different meanings were able to evolve for both women as they became able to discuss the roles of cooperation and communality in African American culture as well as money and survival in Jewish history, and that sources of esteem were very different in their different cultures. Gena then was able to understand both Sheryl's sense of family obligation as well as the importance of maintaining a high profile personal style through wearing fashionable clothes.

Sheryl's and Gena's relationship had many strengths. They genuinely liked each other, enjoyed each other's company, shared many similar interests and communicated honestly and directly, often with a sharp and teasing wit. In addition, they maintained a strong sexual attraction which was an important part of their relationship. However, although therapy helped each one understand the other better and anger and resentment did decrease, their individual needs took precedence and they decided to live apart. However, both hoped they could eventually learn to accept and negotiate their many differences and planned to seek additional social support through locating other mixed-race lesbian couples.

TWO CULTURES/ONE RELATIONSHIP

A bird may love a fish, but where would they build a home together?

—From *Fiddler on the Roof*

Julia, Susan, Sheryl, and Gena demonstrate many of the dilemmas and difficulties which interracial lesbian couples face. Each couple has had to manage multiple differences including class of origin, norms and values about family obligations, time, planning, money, and expectations of significant relationships. Julia and Susan struggle over family involvement. Sheryl and Gena endure relationship invalidation, family of origin antagonisms, and limited connection to their lesbian community so that they are thrown back on each other for most social activities and support.

Each couple has encountered interracial relationship prejudice and has learned to talk openly about race, racism and the many adjustments required in order to be together. Both Susan and Gena stated that they were initially very focused on public self-consciousness and the experience of obvious stares when out with Julia and Sheryl, and still believe that their racial difference "outs" them as lesbians. In addition, both women learned sensitivity to their partner's assessments and feelings as to what areas and neighborhoods were comfortable and safe for Hispanic and African American people. Gena was especially concerned about Sheryl's level of comfort as she was frequently the only woman of color at lesbian social gatherings.

Both Susan and Gena expressed that it had taken them many years to understand the degree of race privilege they had as white women and felt they had learned first-hand the pervasiveness and destructiveness of racism. As Gena stated, "I never knew it was a privilege to be able to call the police." All four women were very thoughtful about their choice of a partner of a different race. Sheryl openly wondered if her preference for white women and attraction to Gena had to do with internalized racism. Julia and Sheryl each expressed anger towards their partners and feared losing themselves (and their communities of origin) by being in a relationship with a white woman. To Sheryl, "You get all this racist stuff in the streets and everywhere it's white, but she's white and lives in my home." Julia spoke of her anger at Susan's entitled demands that her family speak English, saying it would have been easier to be with a Spanish woman who would understand the situation.

Julia and Sheryl believed also that their partners' lives would have been easier if they were with white women and that they had exposed them to a very different kind of world in terms of scope of problems which included violence (Julia's brother-in-law is in prison and one of Sheryl's nephews is confined to a wheelchair due to a gunshot wound).

However, each woman stated her appreciation of their cultural differences, expressing how they had expanded culturally, and how much they enjoyed participating in different social customs. In addition, all articulated a complementary attraction towards their partner (Burch, 1993) who seemed to fill in what was undeveloped in themselves. Gena enjoyed Sheryl's "street wise" directness. Susan, who tended towards formality and constraint, loved Julia's expressiveness and confessed to envying her close family relationships. Julia, in turn, admired what she called Susan's "sophistication." Also, although understanding its race/class underpinnings, both Julia and Sheryl appreciated their partner's ability to represent them and negotiate comfortably in interactions with the larger culture or white world. In addition, all four women expressed that they believed their physical differences heightened eroticism, sexual attraction and desire.

When race and class are added to the clinical lens, only then are clinicians in a position to observe those relational dynamics and conflicts which originate in cultural differences and to understand and clarify their impact on the relationship. Thus, the race/class sensitive clinician can articulate perspectives which reframe power struggles and the personalizing of difference and disclose other meanings. Moreover, she has the opportunity and the privilege to offer validation of attraction to difference and serve to affirm both cultural enrichment and expansion when intimacy is joined to cultural difference.

REFERENCES

Burch, B. (1993). *On intimate terms: The psychology of difference in lesbian relationships.* Urbana IL: Univ. of Illinois Press.
Burch, B. (1987). Barriers to intimacy: Conflicts over power, dependency, and nurturing in lesbian relationships. In Boston Lesbian Psychologies Book Collective (Ed.), *Lesbian psychologies: Explorations and challenges* (pp. 126-141). Champaign, IL: Univ. of Illinois Press.
Burnette, E. (1995, September). The strengths of mixed-race relationships. *APA Monitor,* pp. 41-42.
Kadi, J. (1993). Love, space aliens and politics. In J. Hardy (Ed.), *Sister Stranger: Lesbians loving across the lines* (pp. 90-98). Pittsburgh: Sidewalk Revolution Press.
Krestan, J. & Bepko, C. (1980). The problem of fusion in the lesbian relationship. *Family Process,* 19, 277-289.
Pearlman, S. (1989). Distancing and connectedness: Impact on couple formation in lesbian relationships. In E. Rothblum & E. Cole (Ed.), *Lesbianism: Affirming nontraditional roles* (pp. 77-88). NY: The Haworth Press, Inc.
Rich, A. (1978). Transcendental etude. In *The dream of a common language* (p. 73). NY: Norton & Norton.
Varga, S. (1987). The effects of women's socialization on lesbian couples. In Boston Lesbian Psychologies Book Collective (Ed.), *Lesbian psychologies: Explorations and challenges* (pp. 161-173). Champaign, IL: Univ. of Illinois Press.

The Narrative/Collaborative Process in Couples Therapy: A Postmodern Perspective

Diane T. Gottlieb
Charles D. Gottlieb

SUMMARY. A narrative approach to couples therapy provides a glance at the emerging postmodern dialogue. This article discusses changes in the therapeutic relationship, content, and process, emphasizing a feminist perspective. The client/therapist relationship is viewed as a collaborative process by which hierarchical distinctions are decreased. Externalization, deconstruction, and re-authoring are described and demonstrated through a clinical vignette. Our own evolving story as couples therapists is also presented. *[Article copies available for a fee from The Haworth Document Delivery Service: 1-800-342-9678. E-mail address: getinfo@haworth.com]*

Diane T. Gottlieb, MSW, PhD (Clinical Psychology), is Adjunct Faculty in the Colleges of Education and Social Services, and Arts and Sciences at the University of Vermont. She is Co-Director of the Family Therapy Institute of Vermont and co-founder of Networks, Inc. She is a clinical member and Approved Supervisor of AAMFT and Board Certified Diplomate in Clinical Social Work. Charles D. Gottlieb, MSW, LICSW, is also Adjunct Faculty in the Colleges of Education and Social Services at the University of Vermont, Co-Director of the Family Therapy Institute of Vermont, and co-founder of Networks, Inc. He is a clinical member and Approved Supervisor of AAMFT and Board Certified Diplomate in Clinical Social Work.

Address correspondence to: Diane and Charles Gottlieb, FTIV, 150 Cherry Street, Burlington, VT 05401.

[Haworth co-indexing entry note]: "The Narrative/Collaborative Process in Couples Therapy: A Postmodern Perspective." Gottlieb, Diane T., and Charles D. Gottlieb. Co-published simultaneously in *Women & Therapy* (The Haworth Press, Inc.) Vol. 19, No. 3, 1996, pp. 37-47; and: *Couples Therapy: Feminist Perspectives* (ed: Marcia Hill and Esther D. Rothblum) The Haworth Press, Inc., 1996, pp. 37-47; and: *Couples Therapy: Feminist Perspectives* (ed: Marcia Hill and Esther D. Rothblum) Harrington Park Press, an imprint of The Haworth Press, Inc., 1996, pp. 37-47. Single or multiple copies of this article are available for a fee from The Haworth Document Delivery Service [1-800-342-9678, 9:00 a.m. - 5:00 p.m. (EST). E-mail address: getinfo@haworth.com].

37

Social construction theory and the narrative approach are new paradigms that influence our work with couples, challenging some of our previously held beliefs and assumptions. Social construction postulates that people, as social beings, are greatly influenced through their perception and interactions. Language, in thought and action, is the vehicle by which we make meaning in our lives. The narrative approach posits that we are interpretative beings making meaning of our world through the language and understanding of our stories. These meanings inform our actions within our social context (O'Hanlon, 1994; White & Epston, 1990; White, 1989; White, 1994; White, 1995).

This article will briefly describe our previous approach to couples therapy, which emphasized a systemic/strategic paradigm. We will review aspects of the therapeutic relationship that encompass the process of theoretical and clinical formulations, the therapeutic alliance, and strategies and interventions. We will discuss how we previously worked in a more directive fashion. In comparison to now, we formulated hypotheses and treatment plans with less input from the couple/client system. We emphasized the maladaptive patterns, thoughts, and behaviors in couples. This included an emphasis on the therapist as expert in relation to the couple's systems. We will describe our continuing evolution towards a more feminist framework. We will demonstrate how the narrative approach and externalization techniques are employed in our work with couples. A clinical vignette will be utilized to illustrate salient points.

We work in a more collaborative, egalitarian therapeutic relationship. Our feminism helped us develop a model called "consultative conversation" which emphasizes relational language. "Relational language focuses on the notion that all spoken words are voiced within an awareness of the audience and the meaning ascribed to the words by both the speaker and the audience" (Gottlieb & Gottlieb, in press). In our current practice, we highlight the exploration of the undertold aspects of the couple's stories. These subplots enable the therapist and couple to view from different vantage points the multidimensional narratives of couples.

SYSTEMIC/STRATEGIC THEORY AND APPROACH

In the past, we adhered to a systemic/strategic orientation which guided our couples therapy (Boscolo, Cecchin, Hoffman, & Penn,

1987; de Shazer, Berg, Lipchik, Nunnally, Molnar, Gingerich, & Weiner-Davis, 1986; de Shazer, 1985; Selvini-Palazzoli, Boscolo, Cecchin & Prata, 1980). We developed a stance of curiosity, spending considerable time formulating questions that served the dual purpose of information-gathering and intervention. We believed that systems were problem-saturated and the goal of couples therapy was to uncover and change the maladaptive patterns that were perpetuating the couple's distress. As therapists, we believed that we could assume a meta-position, that is, a position outside the couple system. We believed that this stance enabled us to effectively generate working hypotheses freed from observer bias. We developed circular questions (Tomm, 1987; Tomm, 1988; Selvini-Palazzoli et al., 1980; Penn, 1982), that enabled us to generate a "news of difference" for the couple to understand their situation (Bateson, 1972; Watzlawick, 1984) and, in turn, create new behaviors and responses to these new ideas. These questions shifted the focus for the couple from a symmetrical, blaming stance to a position of openness. By asking questions of one person about the other instead of asking the individuals in the couple to describe their thoughts and feelings to each other, new information and descriptions of the distressful situations were generated. Once we became clear that our working hypothesis was substantiated, we devised (at times, paradoxical) interventions to perturb the couple's system. Throughout our work, we believed that our role as therapists was to determine what the problems were and to plan strategies that would ameliorate these problems. Originally our hypotheses and strategic plans excluded the couple until we informed them of our formulations and interventions.

We became uneasy with the hierarchy that was intrinsic to the systemic/strategic paradigm. We found that our sociopolitical ideology of feminism ran contrary to this power imbalance. In our clinical practice we increasingly acted as skilled technicians rather than more compassionate therapists. Although we recognized the effectiveness of the work, we missed the humanness that is part of the art of couples therapy. Out of our search for a more congruent relationship with the couples, our curiosity expanded towards postmodern theory and narrative approaches.

EVOLUTION TO POSTMODERNISM AND NARRATIVE

We recognize that we bring preconceived ideas into therapy that greatly influence our interactions with couples. We adopt the idea that we are part of the system and not objective observers. Given our belief that the observing system and the observed system are inseparable, we strive to find a language that makes meaning for both the therapist and the couple. This shift from systemic/strategic perspective to postmodernism punctuates the increasing feminist rationale that governs our work. We are aware of the dominant culture imperatives which influence couples in our societies. We recognize the importance of language as a tool that either perpetuates or interrupts these dominant themes. "Instead of focusing on how the couple should change their relationship, we converse with the couple about their stories. We believe this dialogue helps shift the punctuation of the themes and ultimately results in change" (Gottlieb & Gottlieb, in press p. 7). We work with couples to discuss those aspects of their stories that are underemphasized. We are interested in how we and couples have conversations which seem to limit discussion to one of problem description. We also realize that couples bring to therapy a preconception of the parameters of therapeutic discussions. Often couples believe that in therapy only the problematic aspects of their lives are open for discussion.

We became interested in the differences between the problem-determined systems (Anderson, Goolishian, & Windermand, 1988) and de-constructionism (Anderson & Goolishian, 1989). Problem-determined systems are systems which define themselves through the sharing of communication describing the problem. It is the sharing of these communications that defines the structure and boundaries of the couple system. The therapist often finds her/himself focusing on problems rather than inviting conversations about all aspects of the couple's lives. This perpetuation of the communication surrounding the problem limits the possibilities for alternative outcomes. We believe that in an attempt to mitigate against the problem-determined system, Anderson and Goolishian (1989) introduced de-construction as a central process in the therapeutic endeavor. "De-construction take[s] apart the interpretative assumptions of the system of meaning that you are examining, to challenge the interpretative system in such a manner that you realize the assumption on which the model is based. At the same time as these are revealed, you open the space for alternative understanding" (Anderson & Goolishian, 1989, p. 11).

Anderson and Goolishian (1992) challenged their previous assumptions of the therapy process. They wrote, "therapy rests squarely on the concepts of the social and dialogical construction of reality and on the role of conversation and dialogue in this process. Therapy . . . becomes the rewriting of history and autobiography through the mutual conversational co-creation of new stories" (Goolishian & Anderson, 1992, p. 12).

We, too, were re-thinking our theoretical and clinical work with couples which included an interest in linguistics and social construction. The shift from problem-determined systems to linguistics exemplifies a change in thinking to include a social construction perspective. From a social construction perspective, reality is perception formed through many factors including social history, economy, biology, class, gender, and ethnicity. These influences inform our understanding of people and their environment (Gergen & McNamee, 1994). For example, it is not possible to consider a violent couple without acknowledging the violent society we live in. It is also not possible to view a violent couple without recognizing the patriarchal nature of male entitlement. The overwhelming majority of violence in couples is men abusing women. The recognition that situations are socially determined through descriptive language enabled us to incorporate our social/political ideas into our therapeutic work. We find this feminist perspective enhances our work with couples.

NARRATIVE APPROACH

The narrative approach in therapy (White & Epston, 1990; White, 1989; White, 1994) embraces the ideas of social construction, strongly believing that our texts (description) are creations of context of the dominant patriarchal society. Our feminism challenges these dominant patriarchal themes, expanding the possibilities for alternative descriptions. In narrative therapy, we explore the stories of couples. Oftentimes, these stories are recapitulations of the dominant theme that has imbued the lives of each member of the couple. In partnership they have continued each of their dominant stories reconstructing themes that limit their possibilities both individually and as a couple. The subtexts are alternative descriptions of the couple's lives which are often under-discussed or not addressed at all. Through the process of deconstruction, these alternative descriptions have a voice in couples therapy. The goal of this approach to therapy is to expand the possibilities in thoughts, actions, and feelings for the couple by sharing new descriptions of old stories. This process is referred to as the re-authoring of the stories (White, 1989).

Another goal of this approach is to de-pathologize the couple and/or individuals of the couple. This goal can be achieved through the process of externalization. "Externalizing is an approach to therapy that encourages persons to objectify, and at times, to personify, the problem they experience as oppressive . . . The problem becomes a separate entity and thus external to the person who was, or the relationship that was ascribed the problem" (White, 1989, p. 5). Our role as therapists is one of collaboration in which we, together with the couple, explore the alternative aspects of the couple's stories. With our adopting postmodern thinking, our role shifted from one of expert to one of shared authorship of new stories. We find these narrative ideas are effectively utilized through our consultative conversational model.

CLINICAL VIGNETTE

Patricia (48) and Peter (49) have been married for 24 years. They have one son, Sam (22), who is a full-time student at a university out of state. The couple called for therapy at the insistence of Patricia's individual psychiatrist after she was discharged from the hospital following a serious suicide attempt. Patricia is an elementary school teacher. Peter works seasonally as a landscaper. The couple was seen conjointly on a monthly basis for seven months by both authors.

We present this case to describe how we incorporate the paradigmatic shift in our clinical work. Since we also have a history of 27 years of marriage, similar ages, and a single child (daughter, 24), we were aware of sharing a common historical context as couples. Both we and our clients established their connection during the mid and late 1960s, a time of social unrest and change. Over the years, both we and our clients have been attentive to the feminist re-definition of gender roles and relationship.

At the first meeting Patricia informed Peter and us that she had stockpiled pills for the eventuality of suicide. She believed that this was her escape route and that she needed a sense of control and self-determination. We, as therapists, found ourselves in an interesting dilemma. On the one hand, we, too, believed in self-determination, but more strongly believed in the preservation of life, given the story the couple presented. As we understood, there appeared to be no intractable physical or psychological pain as described by the couple. Instead they both talked of times when it was "too much to bear." Patricia's description largely contained one dominant story. "I'm in such psychic pain and so alone that I need to know that I can end my life at any time." Peter, a soft spoken man, repeated his part in that dominant story. He described his sense of impotency to save his wife from despair. Yet, he also expressed his anger that she would not include him in discussion about her plans of suicide.

Our first thoughts were to explore the notion of safety and its meaning to this couple. Since the primary description was one of hopelessness, we believed that alternate stories containing hopefulness might engender a difference regarding safety and self-determination. We described to the couple that we were interested in exploring alternative aspects of their story as a way of mitigating the control that Patricia's depression had over both Patricia individually and the couple conjointly. We introduced, through our discussion, the idea that depression was multifaceted and multidimensional, appearing to control Patricia, Peter, and the couple.

EXTERNALIZING APPROACH

By focusing on depression as a separate object that interferes with many aspects of their lives, we invite the clients to shift their relationship to the depression. No longer is the client seen as the "depressed one," but rather is regarded as the one who "lives with and manages" the depression. Thus, objectification of the problem is the first step in externalization.

We questioned Patricia about the history of depression. These questions de-emphasized her internal despair. Our questions encouraged a discussion concerning depression: "When did depression dominate her, when did it dominate the couple's life, at what point did depression seem not to be present?" This questioning invited Patricia to have depression removed from her sense of self, to a description containing the ways in which depression interfered with her sense of self. Peter was then also asked to discuss his relations to Patricia when depression was dominant and when depression was absent. Through this discussion the four of us engaged in a unique conversation about depression. We expanded the landscapes of consciousness and action (White, 1992).

LANDSCAPES OF CONSCIOUSNESS AND LANDSCAPES OF ACTION

Landscapes of consciousness and landscapes of action are means of describing stories which introduce different emphases from the traditional renditions. White (1992) refers to this as "unique outcomes." Landscapes of consciousness refer to the values, feelings, motives, beliefs, and characteristics that inform our description of our stories. Landscapes of action describe the sequences of behavior about particular events in peoples' lives. We utilize "landscape of action questions [to] encourage persons to situate unique outcomes in sequences of events that unfold across time according to particular plots." We also use "landscape of consciousness" questions [to] "encourage persons to reflect on and to determine the meaning of those developments that occur in the landscape of action" (White, 1992, p. 127). This discussion introduces a re-authoring of the stories deconstructing the past, present, and future. With this re-authorship, couples are freed from the dominant descriptions and given the opportunity to present multi-storied descriptions of their lives.

It is important to note that depression is often ascribed to women. At this first session, we wondered if Peter's quietness was another expression of depression overtaking individuals in the couple. As we found out in a later session, this was the case. When depression took Peter over, the couple was far less likely to converse about it. Peter established a more traditional male position: he withdrew physically and emotionally from the relationship. This is a prime manifestation of a dominant theme in our society (men withdrawing during emotional distress, while women relate and connect during emotional turmoil). Through discussions within the couple therapy, we invite the couple to recognize that their stories are often informed or influenced by the dominant sociopolitical themes of our society.

After the conversation in which we externalized the depression, Patricia and Peter both agreed that to re-introduce hope into their relationship, safety needed to be established. They agreed that the couple would bring Patricia's "stockpile of pills" to her psychiatrist two days later and allowed us to call this doctor to verify it.

In a later session, the four of us discussed their changing roles from couple to parents to couple as the life cycle continued. Peter described his youth and young adulthood as a period of freedom and self-expression. His wanderlust was punctuated by poetry writing, rock climbing, and backpacking. He regarded himself as free-spirited, much in the style of the 1960s. Patricia depicted herself in a similar manner except her activities tended to involve other people. The couple portrayed a change in their relationship upon deciding to have a child. Once again, this couple was attempting to incorporate the feminist ideals of family, in which both genders were actively involved in child rearing and breadwinning. They reported that when Peter decided to leave full-time employment and pursue his interest in landscape design, they both theoretically supported these ideas. Their account of their experience of this time included an increased tension. Patricia described the pressure of becoming the primary income provider for the family. The change to nuclear family with a young child was dramatic. Peter described becoming more withdrawn and distant. Patricia told us about her yearning to be more connected with Peter.

DECONSTRUCTION AND RE-AUTHORING

Through the process of deconstruction we challenge assumptive meanings by taking apart the couple's traditional attributions of their stories. We invite an expansion of possibilities to both the spoken stories and the behaviors and feelings in the future. This is a process of reconstruction in a different and unique way. The re-authoring approach broadens the story to include the sociopolitical context which leads to the formation of new plots and subplots. Correspondingly, this approach encourages a shift from recursive and oppressive descriptions to description of competency and empowerment. We are particularly interested in uncovering the less frequently discussed aspects of couple's lives. We believe encouraging the discussion of subplots in couple's stories expands the possibilities for unique outcomes.

CONCLUSIONS

The narrative approach is respectful and impactful in work with couples. Given that the inherent nature of the therapeutic relationship has a power imbalance, this approach tends to mitigate against this imbalance. This is a central component to feminist therapy. This approach affords us a continued movement towards a more collaborative position in the therapeutic relationship. The focus of this approach is the sharing of stories, told and yet to be told. With this comes the shift in emphasis of themes of these stories. Externalizing, deconstructing, and re-authoring are approaches that we use to facilitate the expansion and development of new cognitions, feelings, and behaviors. The reemphasis on the sociopolitical forces on couples tempers the pathologization of the couple and the individuals within the couple by the use of the narrative approach. The narrative approach embraces the feminist notions of de-pathologizing and challenges the dominant patriarchal influences on couples.

We are reexamining the stories of our work with clients through multiple descriptions and perspectives. We find ourselves focusing more on the inherent and yet undiscussed strengths and competencies of individuals and couples. This shift of emphasis renews our interests and vitality in our life's work.

REFERENCES

Anderson, H., Goolishian, H., & Windermand, L. (1988). Problem-determined systems: Towards transformation in family therapy. *Journal of strategic and systemic therapies, 5(4),* 1-13.

Anderson, H. & Goolishian, H. (1989). Dialogic rather than interventionist: An interview by L. Windermand. *Family therapy news,* Nov/Dec.

Bateson, G. (1972). *Steps to an ecology of mind*. N.Y.: Ballantine Books.

Boscolo, L., Cecchin, G., Hoffman, L., & Penn, P. (1987). *Milan systemic family therapy*. N.Y.: Basic Books.

de Shazer, S. (1985). *Keys to solution in brief therapy*. N.Y.: W.W. Norton & Comp.

de Shazer, S., Berg, I., Lipchik, E., Nunnally, E., Molnar, A., Gingerich, W., & Weiner-Davis, M. (1986). Brief therapy: Focused solution development. *Family process, 25,* 207-221.

Gergen, K. & McNamee, S. (1994). *Resources for relational responsibility*. Relational Practices. Taos Institute Conference, Taos, N.M.

Goolishian, H. & Anderson, H. (1992). Strategy and intervention versus nonintervention: A matter of theory. *Journal of marital and family therapy, 18(1),* 5-15.

Gottlieb, D. & Gottlieb, C. (in press). Consultative conversations: The change process in couples therapy. *Journal of couples therapy*.

O'Hanlon, B. (1994). The third wave. *Family therapy networker, Nov/Dec.,* 19-29.

Penn, P. (1982). Circular questioning. *Family process, 21,* 267-280.

Selvini-Palazzoli, M., Boscolo, L., Cecchin, G., & Prata (1980). Hypothesizing, Circularity, Neutrality: Three guidelines for the conductor of the session. *Family process, 19(1),* 3-12.

Tomm, K. (1987). Interventive interviewing: II. Reflexive questioning as a means to enable self-healing. *Family process, 26,* 167-183.

Tomm, K. (1988). Interventive interviewing: Part III. Intending to ask lineal, circular, strategic, reflective questions? *Family process, 27(1),* 1-15.

Watzlawick, P. (Ed.) (1984). *The invented reality: How do we know what we believe we know?* N.Y.: Norton & Comp.

White, M. (1989). The externalizing of the problem and the re-authoring of lives and relationships. In Michael White, *Selected papers*. Adelaide, Australia: Dulwiche Centre Publications, pp. 5-28.

White, M. (1992). Deconstruction and therapy. In White (Ed.), *Experience, contradiction, narrative, and imagination*. Adelaide, Australia: Dulwiche Centre Publications.

White, M. (1995). *Re-authoring lives: Interviews and essays*. Adelaide, Australia: Dulwiche Centre Publications.

White, M. & Epston, D. (1990). *Narrative means to therapeutic ends*. N.Y.: W.W. Norton & Comp.

African American Lesbian Couples: Ethnocultural Considerations in Psychotherapy

Beverly Greene
Nancy Boyd-Franklin

SUMMARY. African Americans are a marginalized group in American society as are women and lesbians. African American lesbians are marginalized even in the broader gay and lesbian community. Their devalued position in the social hierarchy gives rise to a condition referred to as the "triple jeopardy." They are objects of racial, gender, and heterosexist institutional oppression. As a result of these circumstances, African American lesbians face a range of challenges to their optimal psychological development as do their relationships. This article briefly explores the ethnocultural background of African American lesbians and strategies for culturally sensitive therapeutic interventions. Specific considerations are given to African American lesbians in interracial relationships and those in relationships with ethnic peers. *[Article copies available for a fee from The Haworth Document Delivery Service: 1-800-342-9678. E-mail address: getinfo@haworth.com]*

Beverly Greene, PhD, is Professor of Psychology at St. John's University in Jamaica, NY 11439, where she teaches courses in psychotherapy supervision, ethics and professional issues and cultural diversity in the delivery of psychological services. She is a clinical psychologist in private practice in New York City. Nancy Boyd-Franklin, PhD, is Professor of Psychology at the Graduate School of Applied and Professional Psychology at Rutgers University, New Brunswick, NJ 08903, where she teaches courses in family therapy and cultural diversity in psychotherapy. She is a clinical psychologist in private practice in New Jersey.
    Address correspondence to either author.

[Haworth co-indexing entry note]: "African American Lesbian Couples: Ethnocultural Considerations in Psychotherapy." Greene, Beverly, and Nancy Boyd-Franklin. Co-published simultaneously in *Women & Therapy* (The Haworth Press, Inc.) Vol. 19, No. 3, 1996, pp. 49-60; and: *Couples Therapy: Feminist Perspectives* (ed: Marcia Hill and Esther D. Rothblum) The Haworth Press, Inc., 1996, pp. 49-60; and: *Couples Therapy: Feminist Perspectives* (ed: Marcia Hill and Esther D. Rothblum) Harrington Park Press, an imprint of The Haworth Press, Inc., 1996, pp. 49-60. Single or multiple copies of this article are available for a fee from The Haworth Document Delivery Service [1-800-342-9678, 9:00 a.m. - 5:00 p.m. (EST). E-mail address: getinfo@haworth.com].

49

African Americans are a diverse group with cultural origins primarily in the tribes of West Africa (Boyd-Franklin, 1989; Greene, 1994a, 1994b). This African legacy includes strong family ties encompassing nuclear and extended family members in complex networks of mutual obligation and support (Boyd-Franklin, 1989; Greene, 1994a, 1994b; Icard, 1986), and more flexible gender roles than white and other ethnic-minority groups due in part to cultural values stressing interdependence and a greater egalitarianism in precolonial Africa. Since their origins in America as objects of the United States slave trade (Greene, 1994b), African American women were considered to be property wherein forced sexual relationships with African males and white slavemasters were the norm. African American lesbians share this history of oppression with their heterosexual counterparts.

Today's ethnosexual stereotypes of African American women as not sufficiently subordinate to African American men, inherently sexually promiscuous, morally loose, assertive, matriarchal, and masculinized females when compared to their white counterparts (Clarke, 1983; Collins, 1990; Greene, 1994a, 1994b; hooks, 1981; Icard, 1986) are a lineal descendant of the images created by white society in order to preserve the prevailing patriarchal and racist power structure. This legacy of *sexual racism,* whereby African American woman are projected as "castrating," encourages African American males to believe that strong women, and not the racism that is often embedded in American institutions, are responsible for their oppression. All of these factors are relevant to the circumstances under which African American lesbians develop and maintain their relationships as couples.

AFRICAN AMERICAN LESBIANS

The sparse clinical and empirical research that has been conducted with African American women has virtually ignored diversity of sexual orientation. Compounding this oversight, research on lesbians has focused overwhelmingly on white, middle-class respondents (Chan, 1992; Greene, 1994a, 1994b; Mays & Cochran, 1988; Mays, Cochran & Rhue, 1993). This vacuum threatens practitioners' ability to treat African American lesbians in culturally sensitive and literate ways (Greene, 1994a, 1994b).

Traditional approaches to psychology are steeped in androcentric, heterocentric, and ethnocentric biases (Garnets & Kimmel, 1991; Glassgold, 1992; Greene, 1994b; 1995), reinforcing the triple discrimination African American lesbians face. Heterocentric thinking often results in misconceptions about lesbians, as common in ethnic minority groups as the dominant culture, among which are that lesbians either want to be men, look like men, are less attractive than heterosexual women, are less extroverted, are unable to get a man, have had traumatic relationships with men which presumably "turned" them against men, or are defective females (Collins, 1990; Dew, 1985; Greene, 1994a, 1994b; Kite, 1994).

Bass-Hass (1968), Bell and Weinberg (1978), Croom (1993), Mays and Cochran (1988), and Mays, Cochran and Rhue (1993) are among the few published empirical studies which include African American lesbian respondents. Among their findings, African American lesbians were seen as more likely to have children, maintain close relationships with their families, depend more on family members or other African American lesbians for support than their white counterparts, and have greater contact with men and heterosexual peers than their white counterparts. African American lesbians have been found to be more reluctant to seek professional help despite experiencing greater tension and loneliness, leaving them vulnerable to negative psychological outcomes when they finally do seek help (Greene, 1994a, 1994b).

The African American community is perceived by many of its lesbian members as extremely homophobic (Croom, 1993; Mays & Cochran, 1988). The legacy of sexual racism plays a role in this response, of many African Americans, to lesbians in their families or as visible members of their communities. In addition, historically oppressed groups, specifically African Americans and Native Americans, have accorded reproductive sexuality great importance in order to ensure their continued existence in the face of racist, genocidal practices. Thus, nonreproductive sexual practices may be perceived as a threat to the group's survival, a view Kanuha (1990) termed "fears of extinction" (p. 176). Although lesbians, particularly lesbians of color, do have children, the internalization of this view may make it harder to accept affirmatively their sexual orientation. When this occurs, it must be addressed in therapy (Greene, 1994a, 1994b).

African Americans often have a strong religious and spiritual orientation. For adherents of religious tenets that have Western Christian religiosity at their base, selective interpretations of Biblical scripture may be used to reinforce preexisting homophobic attitudes (Greene, 1994a, 1994b; Icard, 1986; Moses & Hawkins, 1982). Certain non-Christian sects with significant African American membership, such as the Nation of Islam for example, view homosexuality as a decadent European practice.

Clarke (1983), Silvera (1991) and Smith (1982) cite heterosexual privilege as a factor in the homophobia of African American women. Because of sexism in both dominant and African American cultures, and racism in the dominant culture, African American women may find heterosexuality the only privileged status they may possess and thus be reluctant to relinquish it (Greene, 1994a, 1994b).

Internalized racism may be seen as another determinant of homophobia among African Americans. Since lesbian sexual orientations may be inconsistent with the dominant culture's ideal, lesbians may be seen negatively by those who wish to model "normalcy" to the dominant culture (Poussaint, 1990). Indeed, the slang expressions for lesbians in the African American community, "funny women" or "bulldagger women," are derogatory (Jeffries, 1992, p. 44; Omosupe, 1991).

Despite the homophobia in the African American community, African American lesbians claim a strong attachment to their cultural heritage and cite their identity as African Americans as one of great importance to them (Croom, 1993; Mays, Cochran, & Rhue, 1993). Perhaps in part because of this, they also experience a sense of conflicting loyalties between the African American community and the mainstream lesbian community. This conflict of loyalty may be further complicated by the racial discrimination African Americans often face in the broader lesbian community, i.e., admission to lesbian bars, employment, and advertising (Greene, 1994a, 1994b; Gutierrez & Dworkin, 1992; Mays & Cochran, 1988).

FAMILY OF ORIGIN ISSUES AND DISCLOSURE

The African American family has functioned as a refuge to protect group members from the racism of the dominant culture. Because of the strength of family ties, there is a reluctance to expel a lesbian from the family or "disown" her. This may result from varying levels of tolerance for nonconformity, denial of the person's sexual orientation, or even culturally distinct ways of conveying negative attitudes about a family member's sexual orientation (Greene, 1994a, 1994b). African American women who feel supported in their lesbian relationship may discover that support to rest on a fragile foundation of silence, ambivalence, and denial. Serious conflicts *may* occur once a family member openly discloses, labels herself, or discusses being a lesbian.

When discussing disclosure issues, it is important for therapists to know the range in which formally forbidden practices are tolerated within a culture as long as they are not discussed and not labeled. The clinician should not equate "tolerance" with approval, as this tolerance may be predicated on a lesbian's silence. For example, a lover may have been accepted warmly by the family until the lesbian nature of the relationship is openly acknowledged.

Therapists will need to explore with the client the diverse responses disclosure might engender in family members who are unlikely to present a "united front," offering blanket rejection or acceptance. An educational strategy is important for therapists and the client may need to be reminded that just as she did not accept her lesbian orientation overnight, an affirmative understanding or acceptance need not take place immediately for family members either. The client should be cautioned not to overreact to an initial negative response, as acceptance may develop over time.

The therapist may want to help the client decide which family members it will be "safest" to come out to at first since lesbians in large African American extended families are overwhelmed by the prospect of coming out at once to the whole "tribe." The therapist must assist in anticipating best and worst scenarios and at the end of each scenario, help the client to problem-solve about different outcomes. It is important for the therapist to stress that despite their best efforts, the outcome may not turn out to be what is wished.

When treating a lesbian couple, both members of the couple will require assistance in learning how to be supportive of each other during this period. This is especially crucial in interracial lesbian relationships, where a white partner's race may become a focus or the sole focus of the family's anger. Her position as an outsider to the family and to the ethnic group make her an overdetermined target to blame or scapegoat for "turning" the family member into a lesbian.

AFRICAN AMERICAN LESBIAN COUPLES WITH AFRICAN AMERICAN PARTNERS

It is common for African American nonrelated adult women to have very intense nonsexual, spiritual, and emotionally connected relationships, reflected in the greeting "girlfriend" or "sister." In keeping with the cultural norm of extended families, these relationships often result in a family's "informal adoption" of the woman friend. Given the prevalence of these relationships in African American culture, the importance accorded to fictive kin, and because of the tendency of African Americans to deny the existence of lesbian relationships, it can be easy for African American families to avoid acknowledging the lesbian nature of a relationship between two adult women. African American lesbian couples can sometimes collude in this denial by keeping their sexual orientation a secret. Others may not keep the information a secret but still never fully come out to their family members. Other couples may come out to their families without the families' dealing with the issue of the lesbian relationship and lifestyle but, rather, pretending that the lesbian relationship does not exist and accepting the lover in the culturally accepted role of "girlfriend" or "sister." In still other African American families, the lesbian couple relationship is fully acknowledged, even by the extended family. Different adaptations and responses are likely to exist among the various family members.

It is not uncommon for African American lesbians to have children from prior relationships. Because of the cultural tradition of "multiple mothering" and grandmother involvement, African American lesbians who are themselves extended family members are apt to have been more involved in childrearing than their white counterparts (Boyd-Franklin, 1989; Greene, 1994b). When children are involved, therapists may assume that one is treating a "nuclear" lesbian family when the couple presents for treatment. This may be incorrect when there is extensive extended family involvement in childrearing.

Therapy which includes members of the couple's extended family often serves the role of helping to open up discussion among family members on the "taboo" subject of the couple's lesbianism. Timing is crucial and therapists may have to work with each family member individually before bringing the whole family together. Boyd-Franklin (1989) in her book on black families in therapy discusses the impact of "toxic secrets." For children, their mother's lesbianism is often a "toxic secret" which is "known" on some level but denied and never fully discussed.

INTERRACIAL RELATIONSHIPS

African American lesbians and lesbians of color in general have relationships with women who are not members of their same ethnic group to a significantly greater degree than their white counterparts (Croom, 1993; Greene, 1995; Mays & Cochran, 1988; Tafoya & Rowell, 1988), partially due to the larger numbers of white lesbians. While heterosexual interracial relationships often lack the family and community support, lesbian interracial relationships face even greater challenges (Greene, 1994a, 1994b, 1995).

The increased visibility of an interracial lesbian couple may make them more identifiable as a couple than two women of the same ethnic group thereby engendering homophobic reactions from the outside world. It may also elicit such reactions or raise other family members' suspicion about the nature of the relationship earlier than it would for two women from the same ethnic group. Because racism is an ever-present reality and stressor for lesbians of color, they often wear a protective psychological armor (Sears, 1987). While many women are aware of this armor and use it consciously, many are not. Still, it is likely that lesbians of color have learned to correctly identify occurences of racism and have developed a variety of coping strategies to manage it. It is also likely that a lesbian of color has developed these survival strategies in ways that a white woman may not even be aware of. A white partner experiencing the realities of racism for the first time may be unprepared to recognize much less address it (Clunis & Green, 1988). She may be unconscious of slights that are racist in origin and experience her partner's anger as inappropriate. At the opposite end of the spectrum she may overreact and criticize her partner for her "complacency," or even assume the protective role of "rescuer." Her African American partner may find the assumption of this protective role presumptuous, unwanted, unneeded, and even patronizing (Greene, 1994a, 1994b).

A white partner may also feel guilty about racism and attempt to compensate her African American lesbian partner for this, a task which she cannot do successfully and that will ultimately leave her feeling angry and frustrated. Neither partner in such relationships should rely on the white person's politics or intentions as a realistic predictor that she is either free of racism (Clunis & Green, 1988; Garcia, Kennedy, Pearlman, & Perez, 1987), or that she understands what the experience of racism is like for her partner on a routine basis. The African American lesbian partner may need to be alert to her own jealousy or resentment of her lover's privileged status in the dominant culture and in the lesbian community. Both may be perceived by others as lacking loyalty to their own ethnic/racial group and may even feel ashamed of their involvement (Clunis & Green, 1988; Falco, 1991; Greene, 1994b, 1995). This complicates both the resolution of issues within the relationship and intensifies the complex web of loyalties and estrangements for African American lesbian women.

While visible and tangible characteristics and differences such as race and ethnicity are easily seen as the cause of problems, therapists should be aware that problems arising out of conflicts over intimacy, other interpersonal and characterological issues, or individual psychopathology may be racialized or experienced as if they are about the couple's racial or ethnic differences when they have more complex origins in and outside of the relationship (Greene, 1994b, 1995).

Some white women may deliberately seek out African American lesbians for a variety of reasons, behavior termed "pony stealing" by Sears (personal communication, 1992) and "ethnic chasing" by Clunis and Green (1988, p. 140), i.e., to assuage their own guilt about being white, their lack of a strong ethnic identity, as proof of liberal attitudes, or as a result of believing ethnosexual stereotypes of African American lesbians as less sexually inhibited than their white counterparts (Greene, 1994b). An ethnic chaser may also seek, usually unconsciously, to gain from an African American lesbian whatever they perceive to be lacking in themselves. This attempt at self-repair is doomed to fail, and the white partner may respond by feeling angry, resentful, and somehow betrayed by her partner. In treatment settings it will be helpful to assist women in clarifying their expectations of relationships beyond a general assessment. The kinds of assumptions held about ethnic or white women within an intimate relationship should be explored (Greene, 1994a, 1994b).

Choices of partners and feelings about those choices may, but do not automatically, reflect an individual's personal conflicts about racial, ethnic or personal identity. When such conflicts are present they may be expressed by African American lesbian women who choose or are attracted to white women exclusively or who devalue African American lesbians as unsuitable partners. African American lesbians who experience themselves as racially or culturally deficient or ambiguous may seek a partner from their own ethnic group to compensate for their perceived deficiency or demonstrate their cultural loyalty. There may also be a tendency for an African American lesbian in a relationship with another lesbian of color, who is not African American, to presume greater similarities than exist. While they share oppression as women of color and as lesbians which may be important early in the relationship, their other experiences and views about matters, such as their respective roles in a relationship, maintaining a household, and the role of other family members in their lives, etc., may be very different (Greene, 1994b, 1995).

It is not unusual for a member of a couple who is essentially cut off from her own family to be attracted to a partner who is intensely involved with her family of origin. This can be problematic for couples when it conceals an unexpressed fantasy of being included in that family because when the fantasy is not realized, overwhelming feelings of exclusion and rejection can result.

A therapist needs to be aware of a wide range of clinical possibilities when treating African American lesbians and not presume that participation in an interracial relationship is an expression of cultural or racial self-hate in the African American lesbian; or conversely, that intraracial relationships are anchored in either loyalty or respect for that culture (Greene, 1994b).

One of the most important aspects of treatment with lesbian couples, whether interracial or intraracial, is helping the couple to nurture each other and their relationship while complex family dynamics are being explored in therapy. Encouraging the developing of supportive networks, whether they are within families of origin or the families many women create for themselves, is especially important for these clients.

All of this work takes place in the midst of many different systems that are antagonistic to African American lesbians and where there is little support for them as individuals or for their relationships. A feminist therapy approach to treating African American lesbian couples must include an explicit analysis of the interrelated systems of societal discrimination against them.

REFERENCES

Bass-Hass, R. (1968). The lesbian dyad: Basic issues and value systems. *Journal of Sex Research, 4,* 126.

Bell, A., & Weinberg, M. (1978). *Homosexualities: A study of human diversity among men and women.* New York: Simon & Schuster.

Boyd-Franklin, N. (1989). *Black Families: A multisystems approach to family therapy.* New York: Guilford Press.

Chan, C. (1992). Cultural considerations in counseling Asian American lesbians and gay men. In S. Dworkin & F. Gutierrez (Eds.), *Counseling gay men and lesbians* (pp. 115-124). Alexandria, VA: American Association for Counseling and Development.

Clarke, C. (1983). The failure to transform: Homophobia in the Black community. In B. Smith (Ed.), *Home girls: A Black feminist anthology* (pp. 197-208). New York: Kitchen Table-Women of Color Press.

Clunis, M., & Green, G. D. (1988). *Lesbian couples.* Seattle, WA: Seal Press.

Collins, P. H. (1990). Homophobia and Black lesbians. In *Black feminist thought: Knowledge, consciousness, and the politics of empowerment* (pp. 192-196). Boston: Unwin/Hyman.

Croom, G. (1993). *The effects of a consolidated versus non-consolidated identity on expectations of African American lesbians selecting mates: A pilot study.* Unpublished doctoral dissertation, Illinois School of Professional Psychology, Chicago, IL.

Dew, M. A. (1985). The effects of attitudes on inferences of homosexuality and perceived physical attractiveness in women. *Sex Roles, 12,* 143-155.

Falco, K. L. (1991). *Psychotherapy with lesbian clients.* New York: Brunner/Mazel.

Garcia, N., Kennedy, C., Pearlman, S. F., & Perez, J. (1987). The impact of race and culture differences: Challenges to intimacy in lesbian relationships. In Boston Lesbian Psychologies Collective (Eds.), *Lesbian psychologies: Explorations and challenges* (pp. 142-160). Urbana, IL: University of Illinois Press.

Garnets, L., & Kimmel, D. (1991). Lesbian and gay male dimensions in the psychological study of human diversity. In J. Goodchilds (Ed.), *Psychological perspectives on human diversity in America* (pp. 137-192). Washington, DC: American Psychological Association.

Glassgold, J. (1992). New directions in dynamic theories of lesbianism: From psychoanalysis to social constructionism. In J. Chrisler & D. Howard (Eds.), *New directions in feminist psychology: Practice, theory and research* (pp. 154-163). New York: Springer.

Greene, B. (1994a). Ethnic-minority lesbians and gay men: Mental health and treatment issues. *Journal of Consulting and Clinical Psychology, 62*(2), 243-251.

Greene, B. (1994b). Lesbian women of color: Triple Jeopardy. In L. Comas-Diaz & B. Greene (Eds.), *Women of color: Integrating ethnic and gender identities in psychotherapy* (pp. 389-427). New York: Guilford Press.

Greene, B. (1995). Lesbian couples. In K. Jay (Ed.), *Dyke Life: From growing up to growing old–A celebration of the lesbian experience.* New York: Basic Books.

Gutierrez, F., & Dworkin, S. (1992). Gay, lesbian, and African American: Managing the integration of identities. In S. Dworkin & F. Gutierrez (Eds.), *Counseling gay men and lesbians* (pp. 141-156). Alexandria, VA: American Association of Counseling and Developing.

hooks, b. (1981). *Ain't I a woman: Black women and feminism.* Boston: South End Press.

Icard, L. (1986). Black gay men and conflicting social identities: Sexual orientation versus racial identity. *Journal of Social Work and Human Sexuality, 4*(1/2), 83-93.

Jeffries, l. (1992, February 23). Strange fruits at the purple manor: Looking back on "the life" in Harlem. *NYQ, 17,* 40-45.

Kanuha, V. (1990). Compounding the triple jeopardy: Battering in lesbian of color relationships. *Women & Therapy, 9*(1/2), 169-183.

Kite, M. (1994). When perceptions meet reality: Individual differences in reactions to lesbians and gay men. In B. Greene & G. Herek (Eds.), *Lesbian and gay psychology: Theory, research and clinical applications*. Thousand Oaks, CA: Sage.

Mays, V., & Cochran, S. (1988). The Black's women relationship project: A national survey of Black lesbians. In M. Shernoff & W. Scott (Eds.), *The sourcebook on lesbian/gay health care* (2nd ed., pp. 54-62). Washington, DC: National Lesbian and Gay Health Foundation.

Mays, V., Cochran, S., & Rhue, S. (1993). The impact of perceived discrimination on the intimate relationships of Black lesbians. *Journal of Homosexuality, 25*, 4, 1-14.

Moses, A. E., & Hawkins, R. (1982). *Counseling lesbian women and gay men: A life issues approach*. St. Louis, MO: C. V. Mosby.

Omosupe, K. (1991). Black/lesbian/bulldagger. *differences: A Journal of Feminist and Cultural Studies, 2*(2), 101-111.

Poussaint, A. (1990, September). An honest look at Black gays and lesbians. *Ebony*, pp. 124, 126, 130-131.

Sears, V. L. (1987). *Cross-cultural ethnic relationships*. Unpublished manuscript.

Silvera, M. (1991). Man royals and sodomites: Some thoughts on the invisibility of Afro-Caribbean lesbians. In M. Silvera (Ed.), *Piece of my heart: A lesbian of color anthology* (pp. 14-26). Toronto, Ontario: Sister Vision Press.

Smith, B. (1982). Toward a Black feminist criticism. In G. Hull, P. Scott, & B. Smith (Eds.), *All the women are white, all the blacks are men, but some of us are brave* (pp. 157-175). Old Westbury, NY: Feminist Press.

Tafoya, T., & Rowell, R. (1988). Counseling Native American lesbians and gays. In M. Shernoff & W. A. Scott (Eds.), *The sourcebook on lesbian/gay health care* (pp. 63-67). Washington, DC: National Lesbian and Gay Health Foundation.

The Use of *Voice*
for Assessment and Intervention
in Couples Therapy

Janet M. Sims

SUMMARY. A method for assessment and intervention with couples using the concept of *voice* and the epistemological categories described in *Women's Ways of Knowing* (Belenky, Clinchy, Goldberger, & Tarule, 1986) is presented. Power imbalances within a relationship are inevitable when uneven skills of *voice* and/or empathy prevail. A case study is used to illustrate (1) the concept of *voice* and what it looks like in therapy, (2) the problems that emerge when *voice* and/or empathy styles are uneven or incompatible, and (3) the connection between *voice* and the holding of power within relationships. Strategies for working with couples having unequal *voice* are presented. *[Article copies available for a fee from The Haworth Document Delivery Service: 1-800-342-9678. E-mail address: getinfo@haworth.com]*

The enhanced concept of *voice*–more than simply vocalized language or a point of view–currently pervades many areas of psycho-

Janet M. Sims received her PhD from the California School of Professional Psychology-San Diego, and has worked with girls, women and couples for twenty-two years. She presently works at Norwich Psychiatric Associates, is Adjunct Assistant Clinical Professor of Psychiatry, Dartmouth Medical School, and consults with local schools regarding issues of gender in education.

Address correspondence to Janet M. Sims, Norwich Psychiatric Associates, P.O. Box 1040, Norwich VT 05055. E-mail address: janet m. sims@dartmouth.edu.

[Haworth co-indexing entry note]: "The Use of *Voice* for Assessment and Intervention in Couples Therapy." Sims, Janet M. Co-published simultaneously in *Women & Therapy* (The Haworth Press, Inc.) Vol. 19, No. 3, 1996, pp. 61-77; and: *Couples Therapy: Feminist Perspectives* (ed: Marcia Hill and Esther D. Rothblum) The Haworth Press, Inc., 1996, pp. 61-77; and: *Couples Therapy: Feminist Perspectives* (ed: Marcia Hill and Esther D. Rothblum) Harrington Park Press, an imprint of The Haworth Press, Inc., 1996, pp. 61-77. Single or multiple copies of this article are available for a fee from The Haworth Document Delivery Service [1-800-342-9678, 9:00 a.m. - 5:00 p.m. (EST). E-mail address: getinfo@haworth.com].

logical thought and writing. Julian Jaynes (1976) posited interior voices as necessary prerequisites to conscious mind. Voicing metaphors such as "speaking up," "feeling heard," "being silenced," have been shown to be crucial tools women use to advance and describe their own intellectual, moral and psychological development (Belenky, Clinchy, Goldberger, & Tarule, 1986). Carol Gilligan (1982) found that moral reasoning in girls and women embodied a "different voice" whose standards were based on care and response rather than laws and rule-following. These metaphors of sound, speaking, dialogue, etc., stand in sharp contrast to the visual metaphors (e.g., "seeing the light," "mind's eye") most often used by science and philosophy (Belenky et al., 1986).

In a study designed to understand how women come to know and view the world, Belenky et al. (1986) were surprised to discover how often women used metaphors involving speaking and listening to describe their experience. The work of Belenky et al. resulted in five epistemological categories which describe the interaction between the degree of silence or voice women experienced in themselves and their capability for "knowing what they know." While most people may not routinely ask themselves, "How do I know what I know?," "Who, for me, is an authority?," "How do I decide what is true?," the ability to vocalize answers to these questions and listen as others attempt to answer them is revelatory. We can hear the underlying belief systems as well as the intellectual and emotional competencies from which people operate in the world.

Beliefs about personal competency and the ability to acquire knowledge are reflected in a person's choices and everyday interpersonal behavior. For example, faced with her new infant's chronic crying, one woman may experiment with many different ways to manage it without speaking with anyone until she has discovered ways that work for her and her child. Another mother may read every book she can find, consult her pediatrician, her own mother and perhaps several friends and then decide on a method for soothing her child. Yet a third mother asks her own mother and obeys her instructions without question. The first mother consults herself and relies on her own authority to sort out how to be with her child. The second mother relies on the external authority of others, but has some procedure for deciding which one she will listen to. The third mother's system for action lies in following her own mother's directions–this knowledge may or may not become her own. These three distinct approaches are both reflected in and caused by each woman's experience with "voicing" what she knows, being validated in her experience and expression, and listening in a similar way to others. The styles reflect operating beliefs that each woman uses whether or not she has articulated these beliefs.

Diagnosis and treatment with individual and couples psychotherapy can be enhanced by identifying the style and flexibility of voicing and listening abilities according to Belenky et al.'s categories. Uneven skills of mind, voice and empathy create interpersonal and relationship problems that inevitably surface when people begin therapy. People who cannot hear themselves think (i.e., hear their own voice) cannot know what they know, much less communicate this knowledge, feel understood, respected or personally competent. Conversely, people who cannot hear the thinking of others cannot genuinely value their partner, much less respect her or his authority.

In any relationship the authority to name what will count as evidence of the right action to take, when to spend/save money, what is a proper use of time, etc., essentially defines who holds power. Inequalities in power (even temporary ones like between parents and children) lead inevitably to conflict, whether covert or overt (Miller, 1986, p. 12). Marital therapy usually begins with the presentation of some conflict. One thesis of this paper is that for many couples, the conflicts can be traced back to inequalities in power which are a product of the uneven skills of the partners to say what they know and/or hear the other with respect. In this article I will discuss a way to use the concept of *voice* and the categories described by Belenky et al. (1986) to assess the individuals in a couple with an ear for power inequalities. I will also present some strategies which can be used in both individual and marital therapy to address these inequalities.

I have compiled Table 1 from information based on the epistemological categories, or styles of knowing which Belenky and her colleagues (1986) gleaned from their interviews with women. Briefly summarized, the styles are:

1. *silence*–a position in which women experience themselves as mindless and voiceless and subject to the whims of external authority;
2. *received knowledge*–a perspective from which women conceive of themselves as capable of receiving, even reproducing, knowledge from the all-knowing authorities but not capable of creating knowledge on their own;
3. *subjective knowledge*–a perspective from which truth and knowledge are conceived of as personal, private and subjectively known or intuited;
4. *procedural knowledge*–a position in which women are invested in learning and applying objective procedures for obtaining and communicating knowledge;
5. *constructed knowledge*–a position in which women view all knowledge as contextual, experience themselves as creators of knowledge, and value both subjective and objective strategies for knowing (Belenky et al., 1986, p. 15).

The authors admit that these categories are not necessarily exhaustive nor are people always found to be discretely in one or another. They also mention that while they did not do their research with any men, similar categories can be found in men's thinking as well. By knowing where each member in a couple lies in relation to these categories the therapist can both (1) know more about the thinking/voice processes of clients and thereby use language that will be best utilized by them, and (2) set appropriate goals for equalizing voice and empathy capabilities so that power within the relationship can be shared equitably.

"I FEEL LIKE I HAVE BEEN IN A FOG"

The following description is from Anne, a professional woman in her early forties who requested treatment for dysphoria, inability to complete writing projects and growing feelings of self-criticism and self-loathing.

I can't understand what has happened to me. This doesn't make any sense, I know what I need to do to get that paper revised and out to the publisher but I just don't do it. I'm just lazy and undisciplined like my husband says. He tries to help me, he gives me advice all the time about what to do and gets angry when I don't do it. My colleagues try to help all the time but I just can't seem to do what they suggest. I'm letting them all down, too, I guess. There's no good reason for this, if only I could do what people tell me to do.

Anne is bright and an authority in her field, but if we ask "who does Anne look to as an authority on herself?" her comments reveal that she looks to her husband or others to define her problems, analyze and resolve them. She believes others have more knowledge of her than she does about herself. This places her in the "received knowledge" category described in Table 1.

In further discussion Anne revealed that she has not expressed any anger in her marriage since an incident nine years before when she and her husband argued loudly and painfully. Her husband expressed fear that they would become like his parents who argued angrily his whole life. Apprehensive about the impact on her marriage, Anne decided at that point she would not argue with him again, in essence to protect him from her anger. This meant that she could not express any thoughts or feelings which had potential for conflict.

What Anne did not realize when she made the decision to silence herself, was that she had also disabled the interpersonal process for assessing options, thinking critically, and knowing herself. When she could not say what she thought or felt and get feedback, those inner contents began to have less reality. She gradually became less and less confident of what she knew to the point where she couldn't write with confidence either. Access to self-awareness had obviously been silenced. As Belenky et al. (1986) put it, "Injunctions against articulating needs, feelings, experiences must constrain the development of hearts and minds, because it is through speaking and listening that we develop our capacity to talk and to think things through"(p. 167).

Anne once had a clear voice and gradually lost it through her decision to protect her husband. I recognized the need to renegotiate this aspect of the marriage but suggested that Anne do some indi-

TABLE 1. Epistemological Categories and Voice Styles

Voice/Knowledge Category	Epistemological Stance (How do you know what you know)	Concept of Self/Voice	Typical Responses to Request for Help
1. Silent	• External authorities know "the truth" and are all-powerful • Authorities speak "at you" to deliver "the truth" or "right way" • Knowing independently is impossible; only choice is to obey or defy authority	• Incapable of learning from words of others • No need for symbolic language. No dialogue with others to practice listening, understanding • No coherent self-image, locational stance only, e.g., "I stay at home"	• Silence, passivity • "I don't know, no one has told me yet" • "Don't ask me"
2. Received Knowledge	• Truth is absolute; right or wrong; paradox inconceivable • Can receive, remember, reproduce knowledge from all-knowing authorities • Incapable of creating knowledge of their own; originality inconceivable	• All-knowledge, even of self, originates outside self • "I will be what others want me to become"; self-description static • Learn verbatim the "right way" from authorities	• "Ask (authority), they will know" • "(Authority) says you should do such-and-such" • "Read this book, (authority) tells you exactly what to do"
3. Subjective Knowledge	• Truth comes from within; listen to "inner voice" • "Gut" is new authority • Dualistic but "right" answers come from within • Distrust alien experience/science	• "I'm different everyday; I keep discovering new things about myself" • Self-knowledge changes daily; period of great flux • Stubborn loyalty to personal authority; rejection of external authority	• "No one can tell you what's right for you" • "You have to try some things and see what works for you" • "This is just my opinion but..." • "You have to make up your mind based on what your gut tells you"

4. Procedural Knowledge	• Use specific procedures for determining truth • Different procedural methods yield different answers • Become aware that "gut" can deceive; like logical constructs either propositional or experiential	• World feels manageable, "I can figure things out for myself" • Hesitant, modulated speaker, careful with words • Identify with authorities from whom learn procedures	
a. *Separate knowing procedure*	• <u>Doubt</u> is primary attitude and tool of analysis • Propositional logic; test each premise before accepting	• Argue positions confidently • Exclude "self" from act of analysis so can stay "objective"; distrustful of emotion	• "You need to analyze objectively all your options and see what is the most logical thing to do"
b. *Connected knowing procedure*	• <u>Belief</u> is basic attitude; empathy as tool to gain subjective knowledge others hold • Experiential logic—"How did you come to that conclusion?.... let me see what you see"	• Interested in facts of others' lives • Use self as tool to see-feel with the other	• "Let's talk about it so I can understand what you are facing—what the issues are for you and what you are thinking"
5. Constructed Knowledge	• All knowledge is constructed—no absolute external authority • Knower is intimate part of the known • Context determines truth • Theories are not truth, but models approximating experience	• Aware of complexity of self due to changing context; "you are asking the wrong question" • Self reclaimed from identity with procedural authority; passionate participation • Feeling informs thought • Value listening/sharing; others' views no longer diminish own	• "What is the context in which you find yourself? Who will be affected by your decision?" • "How did the whole thing come about?" • "What is best at this point in time?"

<u>Note.</u> Summarization using categories from *Women's Ways of Knowing*, by M.F. Belenky, B.M. Clinchy, N.R. Goldberger, and J.M. Tarule, 1986, New York: Basic Books.

vidual therapy initially to regain her voice and some clarity on herself. In the early stage of this work, Anne would attempt to try and place me in the role of authority rather than struggle with establishing her own. Although it would have been easy to offer suggestions, it is more therapeutic to ask probing questions (e.g., What do you think is best and for what reasons? What will happen if you do it that way, what will happen if you don't?) and validate Anne's efforts to discover answers for herself. At this stage therapy for Anne includes both discovery about herself and affirmation of her *capability to learn* the self-discovery process: to listen to what she feels, to listen for promising thoughts, to recognize blind alleys and change course, to learn about herself by her own efforts.

Gradually Anne felt more confident, both in what she knew about herself and her ability to look at issues on her own. Here are some excerpts which reveal the progression of Anne moving out of the position of received knowledge:

> I know there are no easy answers but I wish you could just tell me what to do. I feel like you have given me a lot of insights but I don't know what to do.

> My mind wanders to other subjects when I should be thinking about the issues that come up in here (therapy), almost like it isn't in my control. I don't like how it feels to look at all these things I'm coming to know. I think I always knew they were there but don't like how they feel and so wouldn't let myself look at them.

> Until now I feel like no one really understood me enough to understand myself. My mom was well-intentioned but couldn't tolerate things she disapproved of. Now I am so aware of how it feels when I am avoiding what I know deep down that I can't do it for very long anymore. I need to know, even if I can't really fix things, knowing is better than feeling dumb. I feel like I have been in a fog.

> It's so nice to know I can trust my gut feelings–once I locate them!

Anne became clearer on her own feelings and thoughts and knew eventually she would have to share her emerging knowledge with her husband. She could no longer stay silent to protect him but was afraid that speaking up would destroy the marriage. She was also afraid that his preference for rationality and avoidance of emotion would prevent him from accepting her feelings as well. His fear of emotion had silenced her once before and she didn't want to lose her voice again. Finally, she could imagine accepting the validity of her feelings and thoughts even if he disagreed. He was no longer the authority who spoke inside her head and decided what was important and valid. She had her own authority and the question was whether they could have a relationship of shared values, which included both rational analysis as well as the feelings which inform any passionate engagement in life. More effective at work and personally happier, Anne terminated individual treatment at this point but felt unready to face her husband directly in conjoint therapy.

BUT THE SOLUTIONS ARE JUST SO CLEAR!

A number of months after terminating individual therapy, Anne and her husband, Rick, returned for marital therapy at his request. The precipitating factor was Anne's frequent refusal to have sex and Rick's insistence that something (i.e., Anne) had to change or the marriage was doomed. In the intervening months Anne had become more and more vocal about her feelings and needs in the marriage. Inevitably there was more conflict and arguing than had been present during the period when Anne internalized everything to protect the marriage and Rick.

Rick is a year younger than Anne, has a doctoral degree and teaches in a technical field funded by government contracts. Rick is indeed a very rational, logical person who was accustomed to being an authority and lecturing students. Until recently this style had prevailed in his marriage also, but as Anne grew more personally authoritative, she had come to resent his monologues. She felt he didn't listen to her perspective and that his manner of offering input was invasive, judgmental, and unsolicited in areas she considered none of his business (e.g., work habits, eating and exercise choices, etc.). Her resentment was being expressed in reduced sexual desire and unwillingness to have a sexual relationship on Rick's terms. Individual therapy had helped her find a voice and move from seeing Rick as the only source of knowledge to herself as a coauthor of their relationship. As she listened more carefully to her own feelings, she found herself put off by his autocratic behavior. She was moving to equalize the balance of power in the relationship, a change Rick neither authorized nor was prepared for. This was his response:

> I don't understand what the matter is. Things have only gotten worse since she came for treatment of her depression and work problems. All of a sudden we're arguing all the time and she never wants sex anymore. I have never believed in all this therapy business and this has only proven my point. The solution to her situation was so clear, she needed more discipline— in her work, her exercise program, everywhere. I helped her analyze the situation many times but she never could follow through with what was the obvious and most logical thing to do.

If we look at categories in Table 1 we see that Rick is definitely not silent nor behaving as the mindless recipient of other people's knowledge. His references to logical analysis reveal him to be a procedural (separate) knower who operates by standing outside of the subject he is analyzing. The problem is twofold: (1) the subject of Rick's analysis–human beings in general and Anne in particular– is not knowable via the procedure of objective analysis alone, and (2) Rick does not have alternate procedural knowledge or skills, i.e., empathy and listening, to approach his subject more completely. He keeps using the same analytic tools (whether they work or not) because they are the only ones he knows and feels comfortable with. He removes himself from his topic to reduce distraction from personal opinions or feelings, as opposed to empathic learning by "dwelling in" the subject as fully as possible (Belenky et al., 1986; Polanyi, 1958; Sims, 1989).

Rick's detached perspective about his partner worked well as long as she was willing to be a passive subject who accepted his analysis about her. Her self-imposed silence had undermined her sense of confidence in what she knew, thus making Rick's authoritative pronouncements even more persuasive. But as Anne gained a self-awareness not informed by him, Rick's observations, accurate on some level but reflecting no empathic awareness of what she experienced, began to feel invasive and presumptuous. His empathic shortcomings also left him in the dark about what was making Anne resentful–he was merely trying to help her as he always had done and in a manner she had often solicited. He had no idea his input was being received negatively nor the reason why.

The conjoint sessions had several goals. First, the differences of their two styles of knowing were allowed to emerge, be observed, explored and validated by the therapist. Second, support was provided for Anne as she practiced voicing what she knew to Rick, and she was prevented from returning to the habit of looking to other authorities when she lacked confidence in what she was saying. Finally, Rick was given practice listening more carefully to what Anne was saying without immediately dismissing the emotional component. This was difficult for Rick because his scientific training had taught him to doubt emotion and he hadn't learned to value empathy as a skill for learning about people and himself. He now had to pay attention to his own reactions and feelings and integrate them with reason–this was new for him. He was rewarded, however, by Anne's natural response of desiring intimacy with him when she felt understood.

Another difficulty for Rick was that it was the political fact that the power base was shifting whether he approved or not. In this context "power" means the ability to influence or control what courses of action will take place and the way the couple describes the events of their lives (i.e., what behavior means, what activity is valid, what explanations are acceptable, etc.). Anne was not willing to be without equal power to guide their discourse but that meant Rick had to share what had been his sole domain. Such a change reflects a marked shift in the balance of power within a relationship and is accompanied by marked reactions from both parties. Accomplishing this shift without blaming either party and without coming across judgementally is part of the skill of couples therapy. Some specifics I used with Rick and which can be applied generally are shared in the next section on strategies.

There is not space here to address it fully, but I must emphasize therapist caution when a shift takes place to equalize power in a relationship. The possibility of violence is quite real, especially if the partner who is losing some measure of control has self-centered and self-righteous expectations regarding the primacy of his or her needs (Gondolf, 1993). The partner gaining in power may then react to the change by abandoning the gain. Rick did not become violent but did respond to the loss of control by giving an ultimatum to Anne about sex–either she would continue to have sex (enjoying it or not) at a frequency he mandated or he would not continue couples therapy. With much fear for the relationship, Anne refused to consent to his ultimatum–for this couple it was a turning point. Rick heard himself make a demand that he would not have wanted made to him and realized it was not fair:

> Things were so different from how they had always been. Sex had always been a critical part of the relationship for me, for how I felt about myself, I couldn't believe she could just stop it like that, I couldn't let her. I felt like she was controlling me and it had to stop. It was very painful but I finally realized she was trying to control herself, her own body. But I need her body, too, and want her to want mine, not feel repelled by me. This has been a very painful process and I can't say I understand it completely.

We can hear Rick's thinking change as he begins to face the fact that he must treat Anne as an equal–not someone he controls or lectures to. It is a classic stereotype for men that women hold out sex as a manipulation or bargaining chip to get their way, and Rick felt this way at first. But gradually he understood that Anne was not withholding sex she really wanted in order to make him submit, rather her desire for sex dwindled with the inequality in their relationship. Her growing sense of personal authority made her able to honor these dwindling feelings by refusing to have unwanted sex.

As he accepted the fact that he and Anne must share control of their sex lives, Rick realized also that in general he needed to include Anne's perspective in their decision-making rather than lecture to her or make pronouncements or demands. He also had to learn to tolerate the fact that sharing meant they would have more conflict and occasional anger, and that this was an acceptable price for a more democratic relationship. Anne had to practice saying what was on her mind and not feel crushed if Rick disagreed strongly at times. Anne also had to face squarely her own ambivalence about work, exercise, and food, as Rick ceased giving her instructions in these areas.

STRATEGIES FOR DEVELOPING A VOICE

It has been shown that development of self and mind (and ultimately equality between partners) is intimately connected to being able to say what one knows, be understood as well as understand what is being said by others. Interruptions in this dialogue or obstacles to the process of expression and affirmation can be addressed systematically in both individual and marital therapy.

Identifying Voice and Empathy

In the initial stages of therapy the therapist listens (using Belenky's categories) for the style of voice used by the client(s). Empathic abilities must also be noted. These observations take place in the first few sessions and in couples therapy are facilitated if the therapist assigns a cooperative task in the session to observe their interaction. In some cases the clients' voicing and empathic skills emerge spontaneously as they describe their presenting problem:

Let him talk, I'm not good at saying things.   (silent)

I can only speak for myself . . .   (subjective)

If only we could really hear each other's viewpoints;
understand how the other one came to see things
the way they do, I think we could probably live with
the differences rather than criticize each other.   (constructed
                                                                                   knowledge)

In other cases the therapist must elicit the information she needs:

How do you decide which one is true?

Who/what has the authority to change your mind?

How is it you feel so certain about that and not about X?

Could you tell me what you understood him to mean by that?

Naturally, people don't always fall neatly into prescribed categories, but once the therapist is familiar with the five styles of knowing it is fairly easy to hear cues to the client's source of authority and ability to speak her voice.

Speaking with Equality

When the voicing styles have been identified by the therapist, the next goal is to achieve a better balance between partners by empowering the voice of the less authoritative member. Depending upon the style and intention of the therapist, this goal may or may not be articulated to the clients. Generally, I am open and direct about what I believe helpful goals would be for a couple and we choose them together. When I am implementing paradoxical strategies, there are goals at several levels operating at once and I may not articulate them all. Developing more vocal balance between partners always includes careful listening, asking questions to open the conversation further, exploration and risk-taking, showing as much interest in confusion and half-articulated ideas as eloquent understandings. The therapist is midwife to the birth of a voice that is at once a verbalizing instrument and a representation of the client's mind and self. For heterosexual couples it is most often the woman who needs this help and the man needs help seeing the value of periodic silence and sharing power.

In the beginning of this balancing phase I point out to the couple the inequities I observe while maintaining a matter-of-fact attitude. I ask them to look at what the value of the unevenness has been for them, i.e., what is the wisdom in such a system? how has it served them seemingly well and been adaptive? Their responses are often that they were unaware of the inequities, or that it was what they had learned from their families of origin and thought all couples did, or as Anne and Rick reported, that such a system was more efficient and less conflicting. In rare cases the couple will notice spontaneously that the unevenness served psychological needs such as enhancing the esteem of the more authoritative member in exchange for enhanced security for the less empowered partner.

I then ask them to look at the cost of the uneven system (e.g., diminished sexual intimacy, boredom) to them as individuals and for the relationship. Men are more often the empowered partners and may have difficulty thinking of ways that they are harmed by having more power and may in fact feel threatened at the prospect of giving up power. I also ask both partners to look at other relationships in their lives and see how power is distributed in them. If it is more even elsewhere, how did the equality come about? If they are routinely uneven, which role does each partner usually play and what needs does it serve? In Rick's case this question revealed that he had trouble with work and teaching relationships, too, that people had complained of his controlling and condescending behavior. This convinced him that there was a cost to trying to hold onto power by controlling others.

At this point it is imperative to focus on the identity and pleasure that being part of a couple provides and that there is a reciprocal dynamic between the individuals in a relationship and the relationship. Life for the individuals improves when the relationship improves and vice-versa. Individuals must make efforts to maintain the relationship in addition to expecting the relationship to sustain them individually. The more the man can identify with the relationship and can think of relinquishing privilege as empowering and improving the relationship (from which he derives identity and satisfaction), the more such a change makes sense to him. For men whose primary identity is in accruing power and individual accomplishments, the prognosis for balancing the power may be grim, especially if the relationship itself is just another accomplishment rather than a person to be related to. The most difficulty arises for men who identify themselves as owners of a relationship (and their partner) rather than as co-participants in a voluntary partnership.

The woman in an uneven partnership more often has difficulty being convinced that speaking her own individual voice is as important for the relationship as it is for her personal well-being. Many women have accepted inequality as a necessary and permanent condition starting with the inherent inequalities of parent and child. They may also fear that such inequality is the only way the relationship can be sustained. Both members may have operated according to stereotypical and hierarchical sex-roles which had speaking and listening unevenly divided between the sexes–men do the talking, women do the listening. Or perhaps one partner speaks with emotion and the other respects "just the facts." The woman may be surprised to have someone interested in her words for the first time, to have her opinion sought, feelings validated. She may feel uncomfortable with the attention upon her, reluctant to speak, fearful of making mistakes, breaking the existing rules of conduct. In all these conditions the goal is to have the client(s) listen for their own voice, listen to their partner, then speak what they know as best they can at that moment. Absolute equality in every discrete interaction is a practical impossibility, but it is reasonable for partners to strive for flexibility in taking, yielding and sharing control of values and events in a relationship.

Practicing Empathy

Therapy must include modeling listening for the voiced member of the relationship. Stereotypically, empathy is not stressed in the socialization of boys and men and in fact may be trivialized (Eder, Evans, & Parker, 1995), so extra attention may need to be paid to teach this skill. For either partner, lack of empathy greatly impairs the capacity to care for and respect one's partner, and makes cooperative decision-making nearly impossible. Lack of empathy has also been related to male violence (Gilbert, 1994), the creation of male oppressors (Eder et al., 1995), and moral reasoning devoid of caring (Gilligan, 1982). For these reasons the therapy must strive to increase the levels of empathy as it empowers the more silent partner to speak.

FINAL THOUGHTS

The ideas presented here raise many questions which could not be addressed for lack of space. Already mentioned is the issue of violence when the power balance is adjusted. Common also is the relationship whose very existence is predicated upon extreme voice/ power imbalances. Should growth for an individual take precedence at the expense of the couple or is the therapist's primary client the "union" itself? Do gay and lesbian couples manifest power struggles differently from heterosexual couples? How should Western-trained therapists approach the power dynamic in non-Western couples? How should therapists approach couples whose power inequalities rest on religious beliefs? The question of empowerment is always political and therapists have a responsibility to be aware of the impact of their own political leanings and respectful of those of their clients.

Therapy which re-engages the discourse through which people think, feel and know, starts a process of self-repair for both individuals and couples. This is especially important when issues of unequal power underlay the conflicts being experienced. Most often, though not always, it is the less powerful member of a partnership who experiences the symptoms, becomes "sick" or generally frustrated with the status quo and seeks treatment. In any case, dialogue is the primary means through which conflict is prevented or resolved if it is to be done without coercion or force (Belenky, 1986). Dialogue cannot take place unless both parties know their hearts and minds, have a voice and the courage to speak, and can hear the other.

REFERENCES

Belenky, Mary F., Clinchy, Blythe M., Goldberger, Nancy R., & Tarule, Jill M. (1986). *Women's ways of knowing: The development of self, voice, and mind.* New York: Basic Books.

Eder, Donna, Evans, Catherine C., & Parker, Stephen. (1995). *School talk: Gender and adolescent culture.* New Brunswick, NJ: Rutgers U. Press.

Gilbert, Paul (1994). Male violence: Towards an integration. In J. Archer (Ed.), *Male violence.* New York: Routledge.

Gilligan, Carol (1982). *In a different voice: Psychological theory in women's development.* Cambridge, MA: Harvard University Press.

Gondolf, Edward W. (1993). Male batterers. In R. L. Hampton, T. P. Gulotta, G. R. Adams, E. H. Potter, 3rd, & R. P. Weissberg (Eds.), *Family violence: Prevention and treatment.* Newbury Park, CA: Sage.

Jaynes, Julien (1976). *The origin of consciousness and the breakdown of the bicameral mind.* Boston: Houghton Miflin.

Miller, Jean B. (1986). *Towards a new psychology of women* (2nd ed.). Boston: Beacon Press.

Polanyi, Michael (1958). *Personal knowledge: Towards a post-critical philosophy.* Chicago: U. of Chicago Press.

Sims, Janet M. (1989). Client-centered therapy: The art of knowing. *Person-Centered Review,* 4(1), 27-41.

Intimate Partners:
A Context for the Intensification
and Healing of Emotional Pain

Maryhelen Snyder

SUMMARY. A case of a lesbian couple is presented in which one partner experienced early sexual abuse and the other a series of major losses (beginning with the death of her mother) in early childhood. The first partner developed an alcohol addiction and the second a high level of emotional lability and some practices of self-harm. Both partners developed dissociative patterns. The couple is now in a committed relationship and have continued in therapy for the last nine months, with sessions gradually becoming less frequent. The therapeutic work has included the "externalization" of the problem(s), some individual work within the couple session using Eye Movement Desensitization and Reprocessing (EMDR), and a strong emphasis on the development of empathic skill through the technique of "becoming" the other person. The case reveals the way in which a primary relationship often surfaces intense unresolved feel-

Maryhelen Snyder is a psychologist and family therapist in private practice and Clinical Director of the N.M. Relationship Enhancement Institute. She is Adjunct Faculty in the Departments of Psychology at the University of New Mexico and the Department of Psychiatry at UNM Medical School. She is Editor of the recently published *Ethical Issues in Feminist Family Therapy* (The Haworth Press, Inc., 1995).

Address correspondence to Maryhelen Snyder, 422 Camino del Bosque NW, Albuquerque, NM 87114.

[Haworth co-indexing entry note]: "Intimate Partners: A Context for the Intensification and Healing of Emotional Pain." Snyder, Maryhelen. Co-published simultaneously in *Women & Therapy* (The Haworth Press, Inc.) Vol. 19, No. 3, 1996, pp. 79-92; and: *Couples Therapy: Feminist Perspectives* (ed: Marcia Hill and Esther D. Rothblum) The Haworth Press, Inc., 1996, pp. 79-92; and: *Couples Therapy: Feminist Perspectives* (ed: Marcia Hill and Esther D. Rothblum) Harrington Park Press, an imprint of The Haworth Press, Inc., 1996, pp. 79-92. Single or multiple copies of this article are available for a fee from The Haworth Document Delivery Service [1-800-342-9678, 9:00 a.m. - 5:00 p.m. (EST). E-mail address: getinfo@haworth.com].

79

ings and dysfunctional relationship practices, and also the way in which emotional commitment and a structure for the couple becoming therapeutic agents to each other allows for a deep level of healing. The couple comments on their relationship process and the therapeutic process as part of the article. *[Article copies available for a fee from The Haworth Document Delivery Service: 1-800-342-9678. E-mail address: getinfo@haworth.com]*

In our most recent therapy session, Nikki sits quietly, almost sullenly (in my initial view) in her corner of the couch. I comment that she has appeared sad or upset since I first saw her in the waiting room. "It's Jan's turn to start," she says.

I have been working with them in therapy for many months. I remember the moments, especially recently, when they expressed joyful wonder at the changes they were observing in themselves and in each other. Nikki had spoken of a happiness and safety in this relationship that was unknown in her childhood and in any primary relationship she had ever had. Jan had said she could hardly believe the changes in Nikki, her energy even in the mornings, her sweetness. Both had observed changes in Jan as well which I will describe below. They had spoken together of the simple gladness they felt in sharing their house, their neighbors, their friends, their meals, their dog.

I had not seen them for close to a month. What had happened?

I knew it was hard for Nikki to speak, but I invited her to speak anyway, to describe what had happened.

The pervasive tone of the relationship as they both described it was "walking on egg shells," feeling critical and criticized, shaming and ashamed. We explored all this together as we always do. The trigger incident had been a tremendous disappointment that Jan had experienced when Nikki didn't do something she had said she would do. She attempted to contain her disappointment, but the combination of Nikki's deep shame about her forgetfulness and Jan's vulnerability to feeling abandoned led to a downward spiral of alienation and discouragement.

It sometimes surprises me how, after achieving two professional licenses as a psychologist and a family therapist and dozens of certificates representing extensive training in as many modalities of therapy, my therapeutic style is increasingly and primarily the style

I attempt to cultivate in all my relationships, a style that includes a deep level of listening and reflecting (Snyder, 1995), an honoring of my own "organismic intelligence" and that of my clients, and the mutual, dialogic sharing of relevant experience, information and skills. The responsibility I take as therapist is to preserve the "container" which opens space for my clients to feel what they feel, think what they think, say what they wish to say, and listen to each other and to themselves.

I notice in this session that although I feel some sadness as Nikki and Jan describe what has been happening to their relationship, I do not feel either discouraged or critical of them or myself. We are together here; when I notice the reality of that I am invariably moved. Here in this little room, outside of which the sky is darkening slowly, we have each other for this journey regarding which we are largely ignorant and almost unbearably free.

Nikki and Jan bring an audiotape to every session (as do most of my clients) in order to record our conversation and listen again. The seriousness with which they have approached the therapeutic process reflects the passion and interest (sometimes latent, sometimes expressed) with which they take on the business of living. Last week, when my seven young grandchildren were all in our home for a family reunion, I observed (once again) that this passion appears natural—but too often lost. These women are "famous" in the sense that James Agee (1960) used that word in his description of Appalachian farm families in *Let Us Now Praise Famous Men:* they have been courageous almost beyond belief. Yet that courage, like passion, appears ordinary in a sense, intrinsic to the nature of a human being.

BACKGROUND INFORMATION

As Nikki remembers her childhood, she felt very lonely much of the time. Much of the family's style of relating included sarcasm and a ridiculing humor. Nikki was sexually abused by a member of the extended family over a considerable period of time. The terror and shame she felt received no expression then or in the subsequent years. She effectively dissociated from her feelings, and even her memories. Anger became her most accessible emotion and, since she was a star athlete, it was often in the context of competitive sports that she expressed her rage, as she says–to the wrong people. Although she was close to her older sister when she was quite young, and although she still feels a longing for more closeness with that sister and with other family members, one of her main coping strategies has been silence and withdrawal.

In this particular session, Nikki describes how easily she feels as though her brain is impaired. Jan describes how earlier in the week, Nikki cried almost hysterically on their bed: "I'm retarded; I'm retarded." I inquire about who told her that. Many people, apparently–but perhaps the worst offender was her grandmother to whom she was sent for academic help on a daily basis. This grandmother told Nikki's parents that she would fail in school unless she received this special tutoring. Day after day after day, Nikki sat while her grandmother both taught her and told her that she seemed unable to learn, at least as normal children learn, that there appeared to be something wrong with her brain, that she was stupid.

I know Nikki's brain. I have watched it blossom into creative thought as Jan or I listen to her deeply and reflect what we hear in the words and under the words; I have watched it remaining authentic and clear in the face of temptations at work to follow certain hierarchical and bureaucratic patterns of thought and action; I have watched it free itself of powerful conditioning to close down, to respond with sarcasm, to forget. It is a beautiful brain. I start to cry a little as I speak of my feelings about what her grandmother did on these countless mornings before Nikki left for school. Nikki has just said, as she has frequently said before: "I do not seem to be able to feel angry about the things I should feel angry about." But she is learning, and it has been a great help to her to hear Jan or myself feeling what she had forgotten to feel–because there was no one to whom these feelings mattered.

Yet, I think perhaps if we had Nikki's grandmother here with us, we would discover another brave and "famous" woman who did not want one grandchild to get lost in the oppression of class. Or, framed alternatively, we might find just another example of the cultural discourses in which we are currently embedded in which image, competitiveness, shame, pride, and various forms of dominance and subordination are the prevailing realities.

Intimacy as Context for Emotional Reenactment

Although Nikki held down a responsible position as a state social worker when she and Jan first met, she was abusing alcohol and most of her friends were drinking buddies. Jan is a lawyer. I began seeing them in the early stages of their forming what has become a deeply committed relationship in the last nine months.

As so often happens, Jan almost immediately began reexperiencing childhood anxiety and an almost dissociated level of hysteria as her relationship with Nikki became closer. Jan's mother had died when she was a small child, and a series of primary caretakers came and went. To some degree her intense emotionality became a coping mechanism, a way of getting and insuring attention that she felt she needed. Over the course of time, she became deeply ashamed of her propensity to jealousy, fear of abandonment, and sensitivity to even small signs of rejection. One result of this is that she has sometimes inhibited expressing, or even noticing, the intensity of her emotions as they grow in strength until she becomes terrified of completely losing control of them–at times, of going insane.

ORGANIZING IDEAS

As Jan and Nikki's therapist, I have used certain organizing ideas that seem to have worked well for them. I will enumerate these briefly because of the limited length of this article, and because I want to leave space for them to share their perspectives on their own process and on our process together.

1. Primary in my mind is the joy I feel (and cultivate) in knowing them. I am continually privileged in our sessions together to receive information from them about how they have transformed each other's (and their own) lives. Two brief examples:

One night when Jan had become frantic in spite of her efforts to inhibit and control it, Nikki was able (as both of them frequently are) to see that what was going on for Jan was very old and, although triggered by something that had recently happened, was not caused by Nikki or their relationship. She told Jan firmly and gently that she was going to hold her. Later Jan said in a session, "No one ever did this for me before in my life!" At first Jan pounded against Nikki much as a baby does when it is expressing and catharting abandonment rage with a primary caretaker (before the later stages of attachment loss). Then she simply sobbed deeply while Nikki held her.

Another example: Nikki and Jan both reported how Nikki would suddenly (as though out of the blue) speak in a voice that was so cold and mean it would surprise even Nikki, as though the voices she heard as a child were speaking through her. Jan was able at times to combine not personalizing this voice with, at the same time, letting Nikki know that she felt hurt and pushed away by this voice. Jan and Nikki became allies in observing and confronting what we called the "meanness monster." One day in session, Jan and Nikki both commented that Nikki had become "unrecogniz-able" in her new-found morning cheerfulness and initiation of warm interchanges. Although this cheerfulness comes and goes, it appears more readily accessible than before.

2. As can be seen, one tool we use, borrowed from Michael White (1995), is the externalization of the problems/patterns that are problematic for the person in their grip. The "jealousy mon-ster" and the "meanness monster" still sometimes want to take away their self-authoring interests and capacities. And we/they keep discovering other "monsters" as well. Perhaps the biggest, most pervasive, and most foundational of these monsters is the shame that inhibits the full consciousness and expression of the complexities of the lived life. The shame is projected as shaming, and in the session described above, it became more and more clear that the "shame monster" had been largely responsible for the downward spiral in which they inhibited themselves and each other.

3. I normalize. Many people who come for therapy, conditioned by the very word "therapy" and by the pervasive assumptions of the culture, assume there is something wrong with them. Especially if they have had periods of feeling strong and independent, or a honeymoon phase in their relationship, they are gravely disap-pointed to see their old feelings and practices take hold again, and sometimes more than ever. It is sometimes new information for couples to learn that a primary relationship will quite automatically reactivate stimulus-response patterns from childhood, and also that

primary relationships are embedded in cultural assumptions that are largely outside awareness. Nikki and Jan have the additional cultural reality of heterosexism to deal with. What better laboratory for discovering what these familial and cultural patterns are than an intimate relationship. In the friendship and commitment of that relationship, it is possible to become allies to each other in un-learning the forgetting of childhood, in speaking the truth, and in authoring the life one really wants. Nikki and Jan have made such a commitment to each other. We often speak of how it feels worse as well as better than living alone to be with another human being whom one is constantly inadvertently triggering and being triggered by, swept into the old "stories" of how one is and how life is. It is possible that both Jan and Nikki were hurt more than the fictitious average person. But their goodness, intelligence, and strength is abundantly evident.

4. There are tools for remembering and processing that we have found useful. One of these is Eye Movement Desensitization and Reprocessing (Shapiro, 1995). Briefly, EMDR is a method in which a particular pattern of eye movement is thought to be a primary factor in helping the client access and process memories, emotions, and foundational beliefs. With Jan and Nikki, as well as other couples, I have been using EMDR in the couple context: focusing on one partner in one session and the other in the next. The supportive presence of the other is both informative and intimacy building.

5. Another tool we use extensively is Relationship Enhancement Therapy (Guerney, 1987). With this tool, which Nikki and Jan practice at home as well, the capacity for deeply empathic (not sympathetic) listening and for effective expression are cultivated. Among the many privileges of working with Jan and Nikki has been listening to their home practice tapes. The level at which they are able to listen to each other opens immense "space" for authentic feeling and exploratory, insightful, constructive thinking. They are unusually competent at utilizing the technique of "becoming" the other which I have developed over the course of the six years that I have taught and used the RE skills (Snyder, 1995). Where they "become" each other, allowing themselves to speak from the other's perspective, they frequently experience the double advantage

of simultaneously deepening both of their understandings of individual and shared meanings.

6. Finally, I consider the use of empathy to be my primary therapeutic tool (Snyder, 1994). I attempt to be rigorous in using it myself and modeling its use for Nikki and Jan. In this context, I am conscious of the failure in empathy which occurs because of my heterosexist ignorance. I have needed to be educated by Nikki and Jan about the unaware heterosexism that I have sometimes exhibited, assumptions I have made from a heterosexual and dominant discourse perspective that simply don't fit their experience and that they experience as oppressive. I think they know that I am open to this education; that I do not assume knowledge in this area. At the same time, I think I have sometimes been able to be a particularly passionate voice for the loneliness, isolation, and abuse of being homosexual within a cultural context that judges and silences that reality. Nikki feels that she cannot tell her family the truth of who she is and of the immensely significant role that Jan plays in her life. Just as I might be able to articulate the cruelty of a child being told she is retarded more fully than a person who has been embedded in that reality, I have sometimes been able to articulate (and openly feel) Nikki's isolation because of her lesbianism in a way that invites her more fully into her own feelings.

THE COUPLE'S COMMENTS

Nikki's Perceptions

I was fighting with not only myself but with my family and society. I thought, hick town on the Texas border would be the solution to what everybody labeled my problem. I took a position as a social worker (hmmm, did this happen just by chance?). I led the life of a cowgirl, good drinking buddies for my man. I was not happy with my script-like life, so I began drinking more. One day the office got a new employee. She was a hippie type, liberal, pro-choice attorney. Was that a stand out in this small redneck town and a stand out for me. I remember the day I met her. I remember saying to myself, "Of course, here it goes again!" I knew this by the tingling feeling I had inside and how I wanted to be near her. Then it started. I started living my two lives once again. After working hours, I would drink and be with her. It was so intimate, so warm, so caring, so right. By day it never happened (that is what I tried to tell myself) and I continued to try to be with men (including my fiancé, as a matter of fact) no matter how repulsed I was. I couldn't let people know the real me, not even myself. So much pain and anger grew inside of me. I could tell I was going down fast, yet denied it.

Then it happened. She left. She took a job in the biggest city and was not coming back, nor was she going to look back. All my destructive behaviors were catching up with me; she no longer was willing to play my two-life game. I thought I had lost her. I, too, got out, yet I took the alternative route. I broke off my engagement and moved to one of the smallest towns. I began working on myself, alone. I slowly worked towards winning her trust. I worked hard on trying to stay sober with myself. We then began couples counseling. The communication continued to grow, the laughter came, the trust developed. Now we deal with recurring issues of both our childhoods in the loving arms of each other. Everyday we grow; everyday we work.

Here is some of what I wrote at that time: "5-19-94; Who has the key to the locked door; is it me or is it gone—forever locked? Trying to find the mystery of the dark. The mazes have thousands of paths. Which one do I take? Constantly trying to find the one with the answers, the one that will allow me to share, to give, to let people in, I run into dead ends, desperately seeking, reaching, looking, wishing that I had the answer. When will the maze end, when will I find the key, when will I find the right path? Will I ever rest, will I give up and end in my own dark mazed world? I crave support, understanding. I want help; please someone help me find the way. I desperately cry in silence, afraid if I am heard the doors will be slammed in front of me, leading me further and further away from what I am craving. I sink further inside, trying not to be heard. When will I give and when will I burst? No lock can surpass the mass explosion. Will someone be there to see me through the mass devastation?"

The therapy with Mel has been very useful. Several things stand out. One time when she used EMDR, I did not feel able to stop my feelings the way I usually can when I notice them coming. I was able to actually cry about certain things that happened to me when I was a young girl. I've felt a little afraid of doing this again, but I'd like to do it anyway. I also remember a therapy session in which Jan started to cry while she was talking to me. When she wanted me to reflect what she had said, I realized I couldn't remember it. Then I noticed that the moment she began to cry was the moment at which I'd stopped listening. That seemed to fit the way in which I learned to stop paying attention to feelings by blanking out everything. Very often, Jan and I both notice how hard it is for me to remember things. I get mad at myself about this, but it helps to understand where it came from.

Another thing I've really liked in therapy is Mel's frequent feedback about what she is picking up from what I say (or don't say). The first therapist I had never did this and, since I don't talk much, it was hard. When Mel "becomes" me or when Jan does it, I feel like I get a clearer sense of what I think and feel. It helps me think and feel more, and it also helps me talk more.

Jan's Perceptions

I first met Nikki in the spring of 1993 in a conservative, isolated oil town in southeastern New Mexico. I was still involved with my then-partner of five years. I turned up in Nikki's town, a two-hour drive from the recently arrived-at home I shared with my partner, simply because my partner and I figured I should take the job offered to me as part of an effort to feel good about myself. Anyway, I would come home every weekend and we would probably see each other once during the week, too. Right?

Wrong. Within several weeks, I correctly guessed that my partner wanted to drop my ass. I guess there is no perfect and short way for me to sum up what came next. I felt alone. I was alone. I felt isolated. I was isolated. My phone bills soared as did my pleas to my almost-ex to take me back. I wore sunglasses at work in an effort to hide my sob-soaked face. I felt like shit. Eventually, I found my way to a therapist. I got her name from the women's bookstore that was in the big city across the Texas border. Faithfully, after work—sometimes twice a week—I would drive two hours to my appointment across the border and into a different time zone. Then, just as faithfully, I would drive the couple hours back, with Nikki on the brain.

I knew from about the second or third time I was near her that I was interested, attracted. Nikki. What a perfect name for this cowgirl, tomboy. We worked in the same office. Her presence made me nervous. I wanted to stare. I started to go out for a few beers with her and her friends and/or our coworkers. I started to have those beers at home, alone, too. I was getting high daily, alone. Right away, after my break-up, I reached out to Nikki with my deep sadness and longing to feel desired, loved. She responded in kind. Our relationship began in a thick fog of alcohol and smoke. Our encounters were always drunk/high, often sloppy, and sometimes dangerous. Inevitably, when not under the influence, Nikki would deny the encounters altogether as she pursued straight relationships with her boyfriends and fiancé. I knew she was not interested in men in a romantic or sexual way.

I also knew that the drunk and irresponsible lifestyle was not right for me. I figured it was just something I needed to do for now, to get through, and would eventually stop. Throughout the next several months, I struggled to stay away from Nikki and those drinking-leading-to-making-out situations. Sometimes I had more success than others. My smoking did not slow down. I stepped up my running. My attraction to Nikki did not subside. I was deeply moved by her, despite our lack of common communication. She was funny, yet seemed very sad, and very stifled. She acted so tough and felt so vulnerable.

My own vulnerability was obvious. As I got myself a bit more together, I was able to better focus. Goal Number One: Get out of that town and get into a more supportive, positive environment where there were other feminists or, at a minimum, other Democrats. Finally, in about as long as it takes a woman to carry a baby to term, I found—or earned—my ticket out. I got a job in the biggest city in the state (six hours away); a place where vegetarians were not outcasts and women did not require big hair. I was as direct with Nikki as I could be: I would like to continue to see her; what did she want? She did not know.

After my move, several weeks passed before we saw each other again. She had since broken up with her fiancé and let me know she wanted to have a go at a real relationship with me. I was afraid to see her. I was uncertain. While I had not totally cut out the smoking, I had cleaned up my act quite a bit. I used the move as a so-called new start. I told her I did not want us to use substances when we were together. She said O.K.

To my shock and absolute happiness, Nikki agreed to go to counseling with me. I was almost totally focused on her drinking and childhood history of being sexually abused. I don't recall sensing my own need for help at that time, especially with respect to our relationship. I knew I had deep feelings for Nikki but I don't think I really understood how much my relationship with her could help *me* grow. That I could use *us* to help me grow.

I have learned so much since then. Nikki and I have been living together for just about one year now. Nikki has been sober for over a year. I have also chosen not to drink or smoke. I completely agree with Mel's statement regarding the commitment Nikki and I have to one another: ". . . becoming allies with each other in unlearning the forgetting of childhood, in speaking the truth, and in authoring the life one really wants."

I have been in therapy off and on since I was about 13, shortly after I made a feeble attempt at suicide and a successful attempt at getting some help. I am now almost 31. The therapeutic experiences I have had with Nikki and Mel have been by far the most stimulating and challenging. I dare to speak about my jealousy and the horrible embarrassment and inadequacy I feel about it. Nikki's intuitive abilities, coupled with suggestions from Mel, have made me feel relatively all right about expressing this stuff and trying to get a handle on it, so that I don't feel so controlled by it and ashamed by it. I don't recall having cried in therapy as I have with Mel and Nikki during our sessions.

I really like the Relationship Enhancement tools of speaking, empathizing, responding, etc. Nikki and I have some difficulty with this at home, and I sense we both try to employ the skills as best we can when we think of it.

I enjoyed trying the EMDR. I found it interesting for me. It seemed, though, that it really worked well for Nikki. I remember a session where Nikki expressed that the emotions came so quickly that she did not have time to put up her usual armor. She said she found it useful to get past her very quick responding defenses. I wish we had used that technique more often; I hope we will.

In sum, it would be no lie to say that the Nikki and Jan of a couple of years ago are almost unrecognizable from the outside. The changes I have experienced in Nikki are amazing. She is so smart. I admire and respect Nikki so much. The changes in me are not as apparent to me. I suppose I am more successful at feeling calmer, more stable, and more certain than in the past.

I am trying to live in a more real/realistic way. I try to be aware of the myths of the perfect romantic love. I want the real thing instead. The real includes work, disappointment, happiness, fun, anger, excitement, boredom, jealousy, and grumpiness! I am more aware of my propensity to criticize myself, Nikki, and others around me. This is another area I hope to work on with Nikki's support.

Since I have known Nikki, my reality has expanded. That has been a wonderful gift from our relationship.

CONCLUSION

As the months pass in which Nikki and Jan are in a committed relationship, we are all seeing how the laboratory that a relationship is, and that life is, is never-ending. As Jan put it, the myth of perfect love is not the real thing. The personal and relationship changes that look almost miraculous don't last; what lasts is the interest in the exploration and the explicit and self-chosen bond that permits a safe enough container for that exploration, and, as Nikki has put it, allows the opening of locked doors.

There is a concept that I first heard used several years ago by Lois Braverman (former editor of the *Journal of Feminist Family Therapy*) at the Women's Institute of the American Family Therapy Academy: "precious fusion." It is a concept that gives validity and healthfulness to the deep organismic feeling of closeness and interdependency that people may naturally feel for each other and that women tend to give themselves more permission to feel than men. In the therapeutic work I have done with Nikki and Jan, there has been an absence of concern with issues of dependency or "co-dependence." Their vulnerability with each other and with me, their need and desire for deep caring, respect, and emotional availability, has been highly valued.

In my work with them, I have repeatedly witnessed how empathetic capacity and autonomous capacity are revealed and developed simultaneously. For example, in the practice of the empathetic tool of becoming the other person, it is continually clear that that ability simultaneously enhances intimacy and the capacity to maintain a sense of "self" as distinct from "other."

Finally, I would like to share a metaphor that a friend and I developed recently when she told me about the experience of working on jigsaw puzzles as a child. She noticed how two pieces lying side by side would look like they absolutely could not fit together no matter what she did. When she came back to them, perhaps hours or days later, and perhaps after working on other parts of the puzzle or just giving her brain a rest, they would suddenly fit, and their fit at that moment appeared simple and obvious. This absence of fit becomes a problem only because we so desperately want it, or them, or ourselves to be different. Otherwise, it's just interesting. When Nikki and Jan and I maintain our keen interest in the "puzzle" and in the "puzzlers," intrapsychic suffering and relationship conflict are often quickly transformed. The task of mutual attentiveness appears satisfying and intimate in itself.

REFERENCES

Agee, James (1960). *Let us now praise famous men.* Boston: Houghton-Mifflin.

Guerney, Bernard G., Jr. (1987). *Relationship Enhancement: Marital/family therapist manual.* State College, PA: Ideals.

Shapiro, Francine (1995). *Eye Movement Desensitization and Reprocessing.* New York: Guilford.

Snyder, Maryhelen (1994). The development of social intelligence in psychotherapy: Empathic and dialogic processes. *Journal of Humanistic Psychology* 32, 84-108.

Snyder, Maryhelen (1995). "Becoming": A method for expanding systemic thinking and deepening empathic accuracy. *Family Process* 34 (2), 241-253.

White, Michael (1995). *Re-authoring lives: Interviews and essays.* Adelaide, Australia: Dulwich Centre Publications.

From Isolation to Mutuality:
A Feminist Collaborative Model
of Couples Therapy

Karen Skerrett

SUMMARY. This paper examines the concept of mutuality and the implications for the feminist practice of couples therapy. Mutuality, the centerpiece of both relational theory and feminist practice, promotes individual and relational growth and also fosters individual and relational resilience. Case illustrations highlight the ways in which mutual interaction (i.e., greater empathic awareness, increased knowledge of self and other) as well as principles of feminist practice (empowerment) become targets of intervention. The paper concludes with a discussion on how to teach mutuality to couples to enhance their quality of life as well as their capacity to adapt to stress. *[Article copies available for a fee from The Haworth Document Delivery Service: 1-800-342-9678. E-mail address: getinfo@haworth.com]*

Karen Skerrett, PhD, is a clinical psychologist in private practice in Chicago, IL and Lecturer in the Department of Psychiatry at the University of Chicago. She teaches couple and family therapy as a faculty member at the Chicago Center for Family Health and consults widely on issues of women's health and psychological development.

The author wishes to thank her colleagues at the Chicago Center, Mona Fishbane, Judith Hazell, Michelle Scheinkman and Froma Walsh for their thoughtful feedback and ongoing, nourishing dialogues.

Address correspondence to Dr. Skerrett at the Chicago Center for Family Health, 445 E. Illinois Street, Suite 651, Chicago, IL 60611.

[Haworth co-indexing entry note]: "From Isolation to Mutuality: A Feminist Collaborative Model of Couples Therapy." Skerrett, Karen. Co-published simultaneously in *Women & Therapy* (The Haworth Press, Inc.) Vol. 19, No. 3, 1996, pp. 93-106; and: *Couples Therapy: Feminist Perspectives* (ed: Marcia Hill and Esther D. Rothblum) The Haworth Press, Inc., 1996, pp. 93-106; and: *Couples Therapy: Feminist Perspectives* (ed: Marcia Hill and Esther D. Rothblum) Harrington Park Press, an imprint of The Haworth Press, Inc., 1996, pp. 93-106. Single or multiple copies of this article are available for a fee from The Haworth Document Delivery Service [1-800-342-9678, 9:00 a.m. - 5:00 p.m. (EST). E-mail address: getinfo@haworth.com].

Recently, a client remarked to his partner, with great feeling in his voice: "I am my best self when I am with you." His partner was quite moved and revealed that she, too, felt similarly. Witnessing such a moment of intimacy, I felt both humbled and privileged, particularly because it arose from a history of misunderstandings, blame, and estrangement; and followed arduous, painful therapeutic work together. The phenomenon this couple captured, best described by the term "mutuality," is certainly one we aspire to promote as clinicians. The experience of interacting with another person so effectively that each feels respected, valued, safe and energized, and in which each person feels a simultaneous confidence in being both "I" and "we," not only promotes individual and relational growth but fosters individual and relational adaptation and resilience.

The recent theory and research on women's development (Belenky, Clinchy, Goldberger, & Tarule, 1986; Gilligan, 1982; Gilligan, Lyons, & Hanmer, 1989; Miller, 1976; Surrey, 1985), usually referred to as the "relational model," has contributed much to our understanding of the pivotal role relationships play in the lives of girls and women. Much less attention has been given to the fact that the relational model of development promotes the growth of men as well. To aspire to greater mutuality in relationships is not "women's way" but the "humanist's way," with rewards bestowed regardless of gender. Mutuality is not a new concept to couple and family therapists (Wynne, Ryckoff, Day, & Hirsch, 1968). More recently, feminist family therapists have elaborated the systemic thinking behind the notion that what is growthful for both individuals promotes the growth of their relationship as well (Bograd, 1986; Braverman, 1988; Goodrich, 1991; Leupnitz, 1988; McGoldrick, Anderson, & Walsh, 1989; Weingarten, 1991). Mutuality appears to be the centerpiece of relational theory as well as of feminist practice. I also find it to be a critical dimension of couple functioning. This paper will examine several ways in which the experience of mutuality enhances the quality of life for both partners in couples therapy and contributes to each person's capacity to adapt to life stress. Taking this perspective, the process of therapy, particularly feminist couples therapy, can be examined largely as an effort to explore and enhance the capacity for relational mutuality.

MUTUALITY: INDIVIDUAL AND RELATIONAL GROWTH

Western psychological theory has been characterized by an emphasis on autonomy, separation and the power of innate, instinctual forces; indeed, the pinnacle of mature development was thought to be progressive independence. Few theories have explicitly addressed mutuality and the idea of progressive interdependence (Jordan, 1986) as a goal of development. The object relations theories (Fairbairn, 1952; Guntrip, 1973; Kohut, 1984; Winnicott, 1963) have expanded our appreciation of the importance of relationships in individual psychological development. More recently, infant research (Stern, 1986) has detailed the process of the active, reciprocal exchange that occurs between mother and baby. It has not been until the work of Jean Baker Miller (1976), Carol Gilligan (1982), Belenky, Clinchy, Goldberger and Tarule (1986), and the research at the Stone Center, Wellesley College, that describes the limitations of the traditional model for our understanding of women's development, that we have come to appreciate the primacy of relational development for individual development. This approach posits growth through and toward relationships, development that proceeds through relational differentiation and elaboration of connectedness rather than through progressive disengagement and separation. The relational model, which has done much to reframe women's empathic attunement in relationships and investment in connection as strength rather than as evidence of dependence, masochism, weakness or other devaluing notions, needs to be further examined to enrich our understanding of male development and relational connectedness as well. Men and women alike have suffered from traditional psychological theories and their individualistic, dominant/competitive focus. Each gender has suffered from the persistent cultural myths typified in the Marlboro Man and Lone Ranger, the Shrinking Violet and Barbie Doll images.

Mutuality, while not necessarily the primary focus in couple therapy, is always impaired in distressed relationships. Obviously, in relationships involving serious estrangement, high conflict or abuse, enhancing mutuality would not be an initial target of intervention. For those couples, the work would center around helping them begin to identify the differences between growth-enhancing vs. destructive relationships. Typically, in my practice, while couples come in with a variety of problems, they also speak of the search for greater mutuality in their relationships. Often, the lack of mutuality is the presenting complaint bringing them into treatment. However, the words men and women use, the experiences they describe, are frequently different. For example, when I ask each partner early in the therapy what might happen to make their relationship more mutual, it is common for a man to say: "We'd divide up responsibilities for the checkbook" or "we'd have sex more often." On the other hand, women are more apt to remark, "He'd understand more how I feel" or "I'd feel like we were on the same wave length." Deconstructing the different languages men and women speak and identifying the unique meaning behind each description is an initial and ongoing task. While it is somewhat more common for the woman in a heterosexual couple to be more articulate in describing her need for greater intimacy or mutuality, I have seen many couples in which the man is the more articulate in describing a lack of mutuality as the primary problem. Either way, the approach is similar. It is vital that both partners feel that their way of communicating, though different, can be both understood and valued. Despite the different descriptions, it is usually clear that both feel unhappy because they live in a disconnected, isolated fashion from one another.

As recent infant research indicates (Stern, 1983), each of us is born with an innate capacity for empathic relatedness. For example, infants delight in hearing their babbling mimicked, and they respond complementarily when another infant cries. However, over time and under the differential socialization and cultural pressures, girls are driven to become "empathy experts" and boys to become "relational dreaders" (Bergman, 1991). In general, women learn to thrive on relational competence and success. We want to talk things through, hear and be heard, see and be seen. Men, in disconnecting from mother and her world, turn away from the relational mode of being and perfect their problem-solving, task-oriented selves. By adolescence, each gender tends to be poised in different directions in pursuit of self-esteem and fulfillment.

In contrast to the one-person system, which focuses on intrapsychic factors affecting the growth and development of self-esteem, the relational model acknowledges the context, the intersubjective nature of individual experiences and the quality of interaction (Jordan, 1986). In essence, mutuality can be thought of as the relational counterpart to self-esteem. In a mutual exchange, there is an active awareness of the other, an understanding of how one's actions impact the other and an ability to emotionally move the other. Striving to enhance mutuality in a couple helps a man regain what has been "lost" and helps validate a woman in her pursuit of authentic connection.

One woman's comment captures the experience of many couples who begin therapy for a variety of relational problems:

> I find that I'm starting to long for these sessions–not just look forward to them. Even for this brief period of time each week, I feel I have his attention, there is someone else in this relationship in addition to me. I never knew how lonely I was until I had some experience to contrast it with.

MUTUALITY: INDIVIDUAL AND COUPLE ADAPTATION TO STRESS

There is ample evidence of the close linkages between individual adjustment and loneliness, depression, and various physical illnesses (Rolland, 1994; Walsh & Anderson, 1988; Walsh & McGoldrick, 1991). There is also good evidence indicating that individual adaptation to life events such as loss and bereavement, family crises, and chronic illness is facilitated by participation in support groups and by the involvement of significant others (Walsh & Anderson, 1988). The reactions of other people appear to be central to the various coping responses of the sufferer (Luks, 1992; McCann & Pearlman, 1990). But as yet, we have not applied a relational model to examine the systemic dynamics that contribute to resilience and coping. It is important to go beyond the exploration of individual factors that promote quality of life and examine the ways in which an enlarged individual capacity for connection improves both individual as well as relational resilience and adaptation. Case descriptions may best illustrate the ways in which mutuality, our ally in strengthing the adaptation process, becomes blocked in distressed relationships.

The Smiths initially sought therapy for Bill's lingering depression following the death of his father. Bill and Susan were both in their mid-forties, had been married 21 years and had a 17-year-old daughter as well as a 22-year-old daughter from Susan's brief first marriage. Bill owned and operated (with great ambivalence) a deli and restaurant that had been in the family for two generations. The ways in which his parents had controlled Bill and Sue's life vis á vis the family business was a long-term source of conflict and alienation between Bill and Sue. The death of Bill's father, which was preceeded two years earlier by the death of his mother, presented a crisis as well as an opportunity for transformation and change. Bill initially expressed surprise at my suggestion that Susan join us, perceiving her as "just wanting me to quit moping around all day and get back into life." As the only son of a mother who he felt both overprotected and abusively exploited him, and a workaholic distant father he idolized, Bill couldn't imagine the ways in which Susan could help him mobilize. Long cut off from his own internal experience, he looked to others to tell him how to feel and what to do. Of course, when Susan did just that he typically responded with rage. Susan came to the marriage with a history of unmourned losses: an adolesence given over to caretaking her mother who was dying of cancer, her mother's death when she was 20, the collapse of her first marriage, and the recent death of two important aunts. As an only child, she greatly missed her idealized father who lived several hours away. She deeply resented the years of criticism experienced at the hands of her in-laws and their "total control of our lives." Beginning with her mother's death and out of her strong identification and longing to preserve a connection with her, Susan somatized her pain. She lived with migraines, Krohn's disease, colitis, multiple allergies and various recurring knee and back injuries. Early in couples treatment, it became apparent that she was losing control over her long-term habit of self-medicating. Susan was seriously abusing prescription and non-prescription medication.

Both Bill and Susan felt victimized by life experiences. They were immobilized in various ways, guilty and unaccustomed to viewing their relationship as a source of comfort and empowerment. Both struggled with a number of the obstacles to mutuality that I see regularly with other couples. Bill, as the child closest to his mother's pain and depression, used the same tactics with Sue as he had with his mother–tuning her out or trying to rescue her, then feeling guilty and angry at his impotence to "fix" her. Guilt characteristically prevents listening and thus is a chronic block to the development of empathy and mutuality. Susan, who became the perfect caretaker–first of her mother, then of her father–learned to keep invisible and devalue her own needs. Over time, she also lost touch with her inner life. She replayed that original survivor role with both Bill, her in-laws and her children at great self-expense. Like Bill, Susan's insecure self-boundaries and invisible loyalties to family of origin functioned as further obstacles to mutuality building.

The heart of our work, as is the heart of all mutuality building, was to teach Bill and Susan to become more accountable to themselves and to one another. The more each could identify what it was that they needed and wanted, the more they were able to offer an authentic, accurate picture of themselves to the other. The less they blamed each other for their deficiencies, the more they were able to appreciate the genuine contribution each made to the marriage, which increased feelings of self-worth for both. Gradually each was able to move out of immobilization and take action on their own behalf. Susan began an intensive outpatient treatment program for substance abuse and began journaling as a way to learn about her innermost feelings. Bill began some career counseling with the idea of finding work that reflected more of who he was. Both began to break out of their habitual isolation and began reaching out to other couples to develop a social life and learned to identify mutually enjoyable ways to share their time. Slowly, they are learning to view the relationship as something worthy of nurturing and as a source of mutual sustenance and vitality.

The Thompsons were the epitome of the "full plate" couple. Diagnosed three years prior to entering therapy with an unknown progressive, degenerative neuromuscular disease, Kurt was confined to a wheelchair and almost completely dependent on his wife, Anne, his 16-year-old son and 21-year-old daughter. He had had a recent kidney transplant and suffered from cardiac problems as a complication of adult onset diabetes. Anne, a fulltime paramedic, was seriously depressed and totally overwhelmed by the caretaking demands as well as by a family she saw as "slipping out of control." Kurt, a printer and part-time construction worker prior to his disability, embodied the strong, silent macho type—a facade increasingly being compromised by his narrowing scope of control. He expressed his frustration and rage in unpredictable outbursts at, as Anne said, the "very people he needs the most": his family. At the time they entered treatment, Anne was anesthetizing her pain with alcohol and had resorted to throwing things and/or calling the police in efforts to curb the increasingly violent episodes between family members. The Thompsons were a couple whose obstacles to mutuality were more concrete and palpable than is often the case. They were constrained by physical limitations to sexual expression, lack of mobility, energy, time, money and a support network. In addition, they were both weighted down by long-standing residues of anger, grief and poor self-esteem. Anne and Kurt had lost hope in their ability to really make a significant and positive emotional impact on each other. Anne's survival skill was to grit your teeth, put on a smile and keep moving. Blocking honest expression of exhaustion, despair and frustration to Kurt, she swallowed it until she felt like "either exploding or collapsing." Kurt sensed her distance and it functioned like kerosene to his smoldering internal fire of failure, guilt and shame. When this "fire" roared to a heat more than he could contain, he'd pick a fight with Anne over some small detail until she'd explode and the destructive dance led them deeper into alienation and mistrust. They further labored under the particular skew chronic illness creates (Rolland, 1994) since to risk deepening their connection and expanding their intimacy and interdependence would leave them even more vulnerable to Kurt's inevitable loss through increasing infirmity and death.

Mutuality, the foundation of solid relational functioning, appears to be eroded in direct proportion to the degree of stress experienced, as these case studies exemplify. One of the earliest and most significant aspects in my work with couples experiencing illness, loss or trauma is to help them arrive at a mutual understanding and meaning of the experience—whether it be the loss of a loved one, a diagnosis of cancer or the discovery of infidelity. Gently encouraging Kurt and Anne to talk about their reactions to Kurt's illness and the impact it was having on every area of their lives together and apart helped them validate, normalize and contextualize their experience as well as to acknowledge similarities and differences in their own and the others' reactions. Once each felt that the other could listen and make an effort to understand, their ability to send clear and genuine messages became sharper and overall communication was enhanced. Typically, as in the case of Kurt and Anne, this process of struggling together to examine, explore and reach some level of common view is the first experience of mutuality that a couple has experienced for a very long time.

MUTUALITY AND COLLABORATION:
TEACHING AND LEARNING IN THERAPY

How best can couples learn this challenging task of building mutuality in our hierarchical, competitive, look-out-for-myself culture? I use the relational model in establishing a context for the couple to experience "supported vulnerability" (Jordan, 1992): a context in which mutual sharing and risk taking is encouraged and mutual power facilitated. This involves more than teaching listening and communication skills; it is closer to teaching a different way of being in the world. For most of us, it is a big step to shift our focus from that of "how can I best meet my needs and further my own agenda" to operating out of an active, ongoing awareness of self and other's feelings and needs. It is an approach that requires both attention and practice. I find that most couples come into treatment with a zero sum mentality (if you win, I lose) and are in the habit of approaching interactions from a protective/defensive controlling position. I begin by offering an alternative–that each partner has a stake in the other's well-being; your satisfaction enhances mine which enhances yours and so on in circular fashion. I stress the idea that both partners must put attention, time and energy into caring for the relationship as well as the individuals in it. From my experience, it is a mistake to embark upon helping couples tackle the presenting problem in the absence of even minimal good will. The spirit of good will is created through building mutuality.

The idea that enhancement of their relationship may be a greater good than the exclusive promotion of individual gratification and, paradoxically, one that leads to greater individual fulfillment strikes most couples as a radical one. However, despite individual variability in capacities to make this idea reality, all couples in my experience respond with an intuitive acceptance, and view it as a worthy goal. As one man put it: "whether or not we can get there is one thing but it seems so right, a far better path than we've been following." To identify and locate power in the relationship vs. within each individual, establishes a climate of collaboration, an approach that invites the question: "how can we work together to solve these problems?"

A related idea that I introduce early on–bedrock to the foundation of mutuality–is the necessity for each partner to consider their actions in light of the needs, feelings and perceptions of the other. I find the majority of my clients (and given gender biases in our socialization, it is a particular struggle for men) come to therapy with an underdeveloped or otherwise constrained ability to consider the other or "hold the presence of the other" (Winnicott, 1963) for any length of time. When this capacity for concern is limited, one cannot take the other into account in making personal decisions or in taking action. Carol and Bob were a classic case in point. They came to therapy after Carol discovered Bob's affair in the 23rd year of a distant, disappointing marriage. Bob had been wedded to his job for the majority of their relationship. Recently he had been finding more stress and less satisfaction from the countless hours of labor. He expected Carol to raise their almost grown three children while working full-time with him in his business. Carol long ago gave up trying to explain to Bob that she craved a job of her own choosing, steadily silencing herself into a paralyzing depression. Bob, too, had lost his voice; a loud and lively contributer to their sessions, he seldom spoke about his real pain, the unmet longings for connection and the deep frustration in having lost both himself and Carol. Each had become convinced that the other was no longer invested in knowing them as they really were, blaming the other for the painful betrayal and bitterness that had decayed their relationship.

The aim of couples work is (1) to expand each person's capacity for connection and relational growth, and (2) to enlarge each person's ability to be fully in the interaction and therefore authentic in the relationship. Central to this is the establishment of an atmosphere of safety–what Winnicott (1965) called the "holding environment." Promoting individual and relational safety, the supported vulnerability encourages self disclosure, increases knowledge of self and other and ultimately builds relational confidence. The process requires therapists to monitor their own vulnerability that is elicited by this work. Each time therapist and couple risk being vulnerable, we all deepen our sense of ourselves as trustworthy, reliable, relational people and enhance our sense of efficacy. To pretend or otherwise deny our inevitable uncertainty and vulnerability reinforces destructive strategies and robs couples of their ability to learn to weather life's certain stresses and vissicitudes as a pair.

Since most couples come into therapy deeply disappointed and disillusioned with the other and with varying degrees of mistrust, the attitude I adopt is one of curiosity. I tell them I believe all relationships are worthy of study and wonderment, that they are intriguing to learn about (as opposed to hopeless or impossible) and potentially valuable (as opposed to no good, all bad). I offer the perspective that the magic of the early relationship may be gone but that they now face an opportunity to build a more complex, less innocent trust built upon a more authentic knowing and appreciation of the other (personal communication). While I certainly have skills and experience they do not possess, we are all learners in the mutual endeavor of exploration and understanding.

Where we begin, of course, depends on where couples are and the degree of disconnection experienced by each when they present for treatment. All couples need to feel safe and that I have the capacity to both understand and help them voice their pain. Slowly but consistently throughout the work, I teach couples the components of mutuality. These components, which are also the payoffs, are: an increased capacity for empathy, increased meaningful engagement with one another, increased sense of authenticity, increased capacity for action (empowerment) which increases feelings of energy and vitality and a greater ability to work with diversity and conflict (Genero, Miller, & Surrey, 1992). I work to help each partner learn to recognize these signs of mutuality within themselves as they occur in the interaction. For example, when do they feel particularly heard or understood by their partner—what internal signals are they responding to and what is their partner doing? Next, I ask them to identify what is ocurring in the relation-ship at that moment that is contributing to their sense of feeling understood. Inviting partners to role play one another is particularly helpful in teaching empathic awareness. When my client Mary takes the role of Jim, her partner whom she believes regularly tunes her out, she develops an immediate connection to the way in which Jim's ability to distance helped protect him from the continual destructive criticism he experienced growing up in a chaotic, alco-holic family. When Jim takes Mary's position, he can begin to feel her desire for connection and the vigilance with which she searches him for a reaction, just the way she did as a child with a manic-depressive parent.

Increasing couple sensitivity to mutual exchange is frequently carried over between sessions in the form of homework assign-ments. I will often suggest to couples to look for, then report back on, particularly satisfying conversations they experienced during the week or on an experience that left them feeling connected. We then deconstruct those experiences together, developing a unique couple profile that assists each couple better to identify the particu-lar ingredients that result in the greatest experience of mutuality for them. For example, one client highly attuned to her partner's closed off body language which she interpreted as disinterest and/or bore-dom, reported that she risked checking out her perception at the moment only to learn that her partner was feeling confused and uncertain about how best to respond to her. Having the benefit of her observation helped him share his feelings of insecurity and together they explored new possibilities for communication.

Since many couples come to therapy with a long history of de-structive communication–contacts which support one partner at the expense of the other–I work to maintain a very clear focus on helping each person identify the kinds of connections that empower the relationship, connections that leave both feeling expansive and productive. Often partners have long silenced themselves out of fear, shame and uncertainty. Simply risking to speak out from their own authentic and unique perspective can be expansive. However, it is important for couples to know that this risk-taking can also result in hostile, destructive responses, or in other not-hoped-for reactions. Authentic self expression does not always win popularity contests or make things smooth. Under these circumstances, the work becomes helping each person create new options for action that better preserve and respect the self as well as to learn to identify when it is safe or more optimal to return to the relational focus.

Couples also need to expect and then learn from empathic failures, or failures in connection. Being willing to acknowledge and explore my own "misses" with them sets the tone and for many clients may be one of the first experiences of a growth-promoting failure and repair. Demonstrating a commitment to trying to figure things out, thinking out loud with them or working to stay connected even when it's difficult and we're not successful reduces the tendency toward mystification and cuts through illusions of power. In sum, the heart of the therapeutic work revolves around increasing couples' awareness of the forces creating a disconnection between them, increasing their understanding of the basis for the obstacles, and discovering together–therapist and couple as a collaborative team–new ways to reconnect. This builds a more differentiated, reliable connection.

The mutuality of the relational model offers a fitting frame for the feminist practice of couples therapy. Strengthening connectedness and mutuality moves both partners in a couple as well as the therapist toward a transformation of the most dehumanizing, deskilling aspects of our culture. It also appears to hold great promise when applied as a way to promote adaptation and resilience; the more we can assist couples to develop genuine mutuality, the greater will be their satisfaction with self, with other, and the greater their capacity to cope with stress and trauma.

REFERENCES

Belenky, Mary, Clinchy, Blythe, Goldberger, Nancy & Tarule, Jill (1986). Women's ways of knowing. New York: Basic Books.

Bergman, Stephen (1991). Men's psychological development: a relational perspective. In Work in Progress, No. 48. Wellesley, MA: Wellesley College, Stone Center.

Bograd, Michelle (1986). A feminist examination of family therapy: what is women's place? Women & Therapy, 5(2/3), p. 95-106.

Braverman, Lois (1988). Women, feminism, and family therapy. New York: The Haworth Press, Inc.

Fairbairn, William (1952). Object relationships and dynamic structure. In An object relations theory of personality. New York: Basic Books.

Genero, Nancy, Miller, Jean & Surrey, Janet (1992). The mutual psychological development questionnaire. Research Project Report, Stone Center at Wellesley College, Wellesley, MA.

Gilligan, Carol (1982). In a different voice. Cambridge: Harvard University Press.

Gilligan, Carol, Lyons, Nona, & Hanmer, Trudy (1989). Making connections. Cambridge: Harvard University Press.

Goodrich, Thelma Jean (1991). Women and power: perspectives for family therapy. New York: Norton.

Guntrip, Harry (1973). Psychoanalytic theory, therapy and the self. New York: Basic Books.

Jordan, Judith (1986). The meaning of mutuality. In Work in Progress, No. 23. Wellesley, MA: Wellesley College, Stone Center.

Jordan, Judith (1992). Relational resilience. In Work in Progress, No. 57. Wellesley, MA: Wellesley College, Stone Center.

Kohut, Hans (1984). How does analysis cure? Chicago: University of Chicago Press.

Leupnitz, Deborah (1988). The family interpreted: feminist theory in clinical practice. New York: Basic Books.

Luks, A. (1992). The healing power of doing good. New York: Fazcett Columbine.

McCann, L. & Pearlman, L. (1990). Psychological trauma and the adult survivor. New York: Brunner/Mazel.

McGoldrick, Monica, Anderson, Carol, & Walsh, Froma (Eds.) (1989). Women in families, a framework for family therapy, p. 61-77. New York: W.W. Norton.

Miller, Jean Baker (1976). Toward a new psychology of women. Boston: Beacon Press.

Rolland, John (1994). Families, illness and disability. New York: Basic Books.

Stern, Daniel (1986). The interpersonal world of the infant. New York: Basic Books.

Stern, Daniel (1983). The early development of schemas of self, other and self with other. In J. Lichtenberg & S. Kaplan (Eds.), Reflections on self psychology. New York: Analytic Press.

Surrey, Janet (1985). Self-in-relation: a theory of women's development. In Work in Progress, No. 13. Wellesley, MA: Wellesley College, Stone Center.

Walsh, Froma & Anderson, Carol (1988). Chronic disorders and families: an overview. In F. Walsh & C. Anderson (Eds.), Chronic disorders and the family. New York: The Haworth Press, Inc.

Walsh, Froma & McGoldrick, Monica (1991). Living beyond loss: death in the family. New York: Norton.

Weingarten, Kathy (1991).The discourses of intimacy: Adding a social constructionist and feminist view. Family Process, 30, p. 285-305.

Winnicott, D. (1965). The theory of the parent-infant relationship. In the maturational process and the facilitating environment. New York: International Universities Press.

Winnicott, D. (1963). The development of the capacity for concern. Bulletin of the Menninger Clinic. No. 27, p. 167-176.

Wynne, Lyman, Ryckoff, Irving, Day, Juliana & Hirsch, Stanley (1968). Pseudo-Mutuality in the family relations of schizophrenics. In Bell, N. & Vogel, E. (Eds.), A modern introduction to the family, p. 628-650. Toronto: The Free Press.

Haworth
DOCUMENT DELIVERY
SERVICE

This valuable service provides a single-article order form for any article from a Haworth journal.

- *Time Saving:* No running around from library to library to find a specific article.
- *Cost Effective:* All costs are kept down to a minimum.
- *Fast Delivery:* Choose from several options, including same-day FAX.
- *No Copyright Hassles:* You will be supplied by the original publisher.
- *Easy Payment:* Choose from several easy payment methods.

Open Accounts Welcome for . . .
- Library Interlibrary Loan Departments
- Library Network/Consortia Wishing to Provide Single-Article Services
- Indexing/Abstracting Services with Single Article Provision Services
- Document Provision Brokers and Freelance Information Service Providers

MAIL or *FAX* THIS ENTIRE ORDER FORM TO:

Haworth Document Delivery Service
The Haworth Press, Inc.
10 Alice Street
Binghamton, NY 13904-1580

or FAX: 1-800-895-0582
or CALL: 1-800-342-9678
9am-5pm EST

PLEASE SEND ME PHOTOCOPIES OF THE FOLLOWING SINGLE ARTICLES:

1) Journal Title: _____
    Vol/Issue/Year: _____ Starting & Ending Pages: _____
    Article Title: _____

2) Journal Title: _____
    Vol/Issue/Year: _____ Starting & Ending Pages: _____
    Article Title: _____

3) Journal Title: _____
    Vol/Issue/Year: _____ Starting & Ending Pages: _____
    Article Title: _____

4) Journal Title: _____
    Vol/Issue/Year: _____ Starting & Ending Pages: _____
    Article Title: _____

(See other side for Costs and Payment Information)

COSTS: Please figure your cost to order quality copies of an article.

1. Set-up charge per article: $8.00
   ($8.00 × number of separate articles) _____

2. Photocopying charge for each article:

   1-10 pages: $1.00 _____

   11-19 pages: $3.00 _____

   20-29 pages: $5.00 _____

   30+ pages: $2.00/10 pages _____

3. Flexicover (optional): $2.00/article _____

4. Postage & Handling: US: $1.00 for the first article/

   $.50 each additional article _____

   Federal Express: $25.00 _____

   Outside US: $2.00 for first article/
   $.50 each additional article _____

5. Same-day FAX service: $.35 per page _____

GRAND TOTAL: _____

METHOD OF PAYMENT: (please check one)

❑ Check enclosed ❑ Please ship and bill. PO # _____
(sorry we can ship and bill to bookstores only! All others must pre-pay)

❑ Charge to my credit card: ❑ Visa; ❑ MasterCard; ❑ Discover;
❑ American Express;

Account Number:_____ Expiration date:_____

Signature: ✗_____

Name: _____ Institution: _____

Address: _____

_____

City: _____ State:_____ Zip:_____

Phone Number: _____ FAX Number: _____

MAIL or *FAX* THIS ENTIRE ORDER FORM TO:

Haworth Document Delivery Service	**or FAX:** 1-800-895-0582
The Haworth Press, Inc.	**or CALL:** 1-800-342-9678
10 Alice Street	9am-5pm EST)
Binghamton, NY 13904-1580	